Advance praise for *The Glass Wall*

'For anyone looking to seriously understand why gender imbalance persists in the twenty-first-century workplace (and what to do about it), this book is both revelatory and important.'
— David Abraham | CEO, Channel 4

'This is a rich report on what it is like right now in the complex world of men and women working together. Its specialty is that it allows you to find your own recipe for mastery of a meaningful work life.'
— Charlotte Beers | Speaker, Author, former CEO Ogilvy Advertising and former Undersecretary of State

'I wish that this book had existed when I was starting out in my career; the advice is so useful, both for women on the way up and for businesses seeking to develop and retain talented women. I would encourage everyone to read it.'
— Karen Blackett OBE | Chairwoman, MediaCom UK

'It is so important to empower other women and that is exactly what this book does. It gives women practical advice to help them navigate their careers and, ultimately, design their own life.'
— Diane von Furstenberg | Founder and Chairman of DVF Studio LLC

'Fantastic to see a book with such practical experience and common sense at its heart – let's hope we won't have to talk about glass walls for very long.'
— Martha Lane-Fox | Entrepreneur

THE
GLASS
WALL

Success strategies for women at work –
and businesses that mean business

SUE UNERMAN & KATHRYN JACOB

P

PROFILE BOOKS

First published in Great Britain in 2016 by
PROFILE BOOKS LTD
3 Holford Yard
Bevin Way
London
WC1X 9HD

www.profilebooks.com

5 7 9 10 8 6 4

Typeset in Palatino by MacGuru Ltd
Printed and bound in Great Britain by
CPI Group (UK) Ltd, Croydon CRO 4YY

The moral right of the author has been asserted.

A CIP catalogue record for this book is available from the British Library.

ISBN 978 1 78125 694 7
eISBN 978 1 78283 280 5

The authors would like to dedicate this book to all the strong women in our lives, especially our daughters, and the lovely men that support them and us.

ABOUT THE AUTHORS

Sue Unerman

When Sue joined her current company, which in 1990 was a small media independent, as an Associate Director, she was the most senior woman they had ever employed. Now at MediaCom, which has grown to become the UK's largest media agency, there have been two women CEOs, there is a woman Chair, a woman MD, and Sue is the business's Chief Strategic Officer. Sue is also a Council Member of the Open University, sits on the University of Oxford Public Affairs Advisory Group, was on the Advisory Board of the Government Digital Service and is on the Corporate Development Board of Women's Aid. www.sueunerman.com

Kathryn Jacob

Kathryn is CEO of Pearl & Dean, the most well-known player in the UK's cinema advertising industry. She was one of the first women to work in display advertising at the *Daily Telegraph* and has worked at Virgin Radio and SMG. Kathryn has used her experience to provide advice and mentoring to numerous young women in business, and to inform her role as a member of the Government Expert Group on Body Confidence and as a member of the Advertising Association Council, an ex-President of Women in Advertising and Communications (WACL) and her positions on the Development Boards at RADA and at Women's Aid.

CONTENTS

Foreword / xiii
Preface / xv
How to read this book / xxi
Introduction: The Way Forward / 1

1 Ambition   16

Men are ambitious; women are ambivalent

Ask for what you want; ask for what you need / 18
Ambition is a stranger to me / 22
Jostling the big boys / 27
Use the frustration / 29
Feel the fear, then do it anyway / 33
Wherever you go, you take the weather with you / 38

One voice: Tessa   44

2 Creativity   48

*Men strut their stuff; women tend to play it down in
order to conform*

Borrow it / 51
Don't zig, zag / 54
Don't fear failure / 57
Tear it up / 61
Be naïve / 64

One voice: Kelly   71

3 Cutting Through   75
   Men like to be noticed; women like to get on with the work

   Brand yourself / 77
   Speak their language / 83
   Ha ha: be funny / 84
   Shhhh: cutting through as an introvert / 90
   Managing up – and sideways (that's your job too) / 93
   Don't be a doormat / 96
   Be seen / 99

   One voice: Mercedes   105

4 Trouble   108
   Trouble troubles women differently from how it troubles men

   Keep going / 110
   Is sex a problem? / 114
   Sex in the office / 118
   The Conspiracy of the Sisterhood: kindness can kill / 120
   Mean girls / 124
   Know when to back down / 129
   The burnout / 132

   One voice: Rachel   138

5 Resilience   142
   *Men take things in their stride that can seem to throw women
   off course*

   Don't ask, don't get / 144

When to walk away / 148
The secret rules of work / 151
The numbers game / 155
The playbook / 159
Don't take it personally / 162

One voice: Megan 172

6 Anger 173

Men exploit their inner bastard; women hide the inner bitch

Power grip / 173
Odd one out / 176
Use advocates / 179
Go feral / 183
Play the long game / 186

One voice: Gloria 192

7 Karma 196

Women are not in the network of chaps: how to pay favours forward and how helping others helps you

Always on / 197
Be your best self / 200
Make a memory / 204
Pay it forward / 207
We're all human / 209

One voice: Carys 216

Afterword / 220
41 Strategies for Success / 223

Acknowledgements / 231
Bibliography and further reading / 232
Appendix: Lightspeed survey results / 238

FOREWORD

I have been involved in women's rights in the workplace for over thirty-five years. When I started out there were very few senior women in law, and those who had made it were usually from privileged backgrounds and had often committed exclusively to their careers. In the years since then we've seen some change – but not at the highest levels and not in enough numbers. We've been told that it is just a matter of women coming through the system: that it is just about evolution, just a matter of time. We are still waiting.

Let's be clear that it's the system that is at fault, not women. We're perfectly smart, perfectly able and often better at management because of the need to run a family as well as a professional life. So, what's the problem, and what can we do about it?

It is still the case that senior men tend to nurture and promote younger men. Women often underrate their own talent, when their peers who are men are doing the opposite. And when women talk about equality in the workplace it can crowd out some important truths about difference. We've been so cagey about special pleading for special treatment that we have focused on equal treatment. Yet equalisation has almost always been to a masculine norm.

This excellent book from Unerman and Jacob does not shy away from the differences between men and women. It establishes what those differences are, and gives the reader a clear course of action to overcome situations where the difference is real, and has become a disadvantage. *The Glass Wall* does not pretend that there is a level playing field when such a thing does not exist. The authors don't support the status quo, and they don't approve of it. But they don't pretend that either ideology or a few words of encouragement are enough to make it go away.

Instead, they give practical advice to help remove the barriers to women progressing to leadership roles, and essential advice to business leaders on how to stop the talent drain of women in their organisations. The immediate task that lies before us is not to dismantle the current institutional structures in business, politics and law that stand in the way of diversity in leadership, although this is, of course, the ultimate ambition. For now, we need to help more women gain senior positions so that we can make those changes happen.

This is a manual of pragmatic feminism in the workplace that is easy to apply for women and for men, for women progressing upwards at any level, and for anyone in leadership who wants a better gender balance at work, an ambition that is proven to deliver competitive advantage to business. The time for change is now, and strategies in *The Glass Wall*, will make this change achievable.

Baroness Helena Kennedy QC

PREFACE

This book will give all women the armoury they need to gain the most from what they do at work, whatever their jobs might be. We passionately believe that every woman can achieve her potential at work and, at the same time, a good work/life balance.

Not every woman is doing so now.

We've both been fortunate enough to reach fulfilment in our careers, so far. Of course, during our careers we have come across women who don't want seats on the board, and we fully embrace that choice. We also know that many men in senior positions are baffled by the drop-out of talented women from the career ladder. They know they're losing talent, and the pressure to deliver a better gender balance on their board is only growing – but no one wants tokenism.

What is missing is a strategy for success to help all women capitalise fully on opportunities at work, or overcome the inevitable complications that will arise over the course of a career. A strategy that can be adopted by businesses to help level the playing field as far as gender goes, that makes talent the only consideration for getting ahead.

That's what this book contains.

The majority of existing material on this subject tends to advise women that to get on they need to work harder, be more 'superwoman' or try to get their husbands or partners to do more at home. This is more of what they have been doing. Meanwhile men are getting further and doing less.

And husbands or partners aren't suddenly going to change and share equally all of the childcare and household chores. Even if they want to, they often can't as they're trapped in their own gender stereotype at work and can't say no to a late night meeting or another business trip without crashing their own career.

We have examined what to do, what not to do and techniques for how to motivate yourself to fulfil your potential by working better, not by working harder. The secret short cuts to reaching your goal that may seem to come instinctively to the Y and to be a mystery to the X chromosome. It will uncover the tribal behaviours that men have and explain how to exploit them and how to counter them.

Each chapter includes an explanation of our theory, followed by interviews and case studies with women who have made it to the top, and also women on their way to the top, from many different types of career. There's a male perspective on things too – insights into what men really think, which are not necessarily the same as what they normally say out loud. It's not good enough to create advice in isolation; insights and strategies for men are also needed to support a more diverse workplace.

If you're from the UK or the USA, have you ever worked in the other country? The experience can be a surprise whatever your gender. British and American colleagues speak the same language but frequently and painfully mean completely different things and often have completely different cultural expectations, humour and work ethics. Take the price-fixing scandal that materialised in 2000 in the antique auction business, which was a symptom of this divide. (This is described brilliantly in Philip Hook's book *Breakfast at Sotheby's*.) There was a secret agreement between the chief executives of Sotheby's and Christie's to stick to a rigid set of commission rates, which led to massive legal settlements. It came about because those who brokered the deal were sure that the gentlemen involved in the agreement would never betray each other's confidence. It was the old boys' network epitomised. But in America they were breaking the law, and there were people involved who were prepared to break confidences. It was a classic example of Anglo-American cultural misunderstanding. Being an English man trying to break into very senior management in the USA can sound very similar to the gender divide in management on either side of the Atlantic: your sense of humour gets you nowhere; your sporting analogies leave them cold; you don't instinctively get the point at which prestige comes before profit.

The gender divide is not that much different. Just as the USA and the UK are often divided by a common language, so men and women in work are divided by a murky glass wall. We can see each other through the wall, we think we're the same as each other, but time and time again we find that what men think and mean is not equivalent to what women think and mean. As women, we're working in a culture where the former is dominant. But we do not have to suffer from this. We can turn it to our advantage.

The book is broken down into seven chapters that represent the biggest areas of the divide:

1. Ambition – Men are ambitious; women are ambivalent;

2. Creativity – Men strut their stuff; women tend to play it down in order to conform;

3. Cutting through – Men like to be noticed; women like to get on with the work;

4. Trouble – Trouble troubles women differently from how it troubles men;

5. Resilience – Men take things in their stride that throw women off course;

6. Anger – Men exploit their inner bastard; women hide the inner bitch;

7. Karma – Women are not in the network of chaps: how to pay favours forward and how helping others helps you.

You can read the chapters as they're presented, or in any order you like. We've developed some questions to help you identify the chapters you might want to head to first, whether you are on the way up, or, as a manager, looking to nurture all the talent in your organisation (see pages xxii and xxiii).

Each chapter ends with a check-list of clear, practical strategies to work through in two parts: advice for the woman in the middle of the situation, and then advice for their boss. (No, not always a man; we're not taking the gender assumptions that far.)

Although we have interviewed some awesome women, we won't purely focus on 'superwoman' examples – those women who seem to be able to do everything and work harder than sounds humanly possible. Nor will we be giving you advice about being more like a man than a man, and we won't shy away from the darker, truer aspects of how to succeed. We will never make things sound simple when in fact they're really difficult, but we will aim to give advice about how to make the more challenging aspects of working life easier.

The strategies for success that follow are about doing things differently. The status quo has been left alone for too long now, and it is time for change. We need a fundamental shift in the way most businesses work. It is time that businesses looked after their talented women employees to ensure that they reap the returns that this will deliver in terms of loyalty, experience and success. We need change in the gender dynamics of the workplace. Women can reclaim the language that is supposed to put them off and build a constructive dialogue at work. Don't be fazed by games in the workplace; learn here how to deal with them. Discover how the use of humour can arm you for success.

Understand what to ask for, from whom, when and how.

We believe that it is time for women to take their place in the senior management of companies in proportion. It's time for this to be normal. No more waiting. The board seats are available, and it is time women filled them. It will drive competitive advantage. Everyone will benefit.

This book will appeal to:

- any working woman who has met a career block that they don't know how to navigate;
- any boss who can't understand at the moment why so many bright women drop out and give up their careers;
- every organisation (and there are many) that wants more gender equality in senior executive management and is failing to deliver.

Before you begin the first chapter, we'd like to ask you a question.

On a scale of 1 to 10, where 1 means very feminine and 10 means very masculine, where would you put yourself? We ask this because we understand that gender is a spectrum. Everyone has masculine and feminine traits to a greater or lesser extent. Understanding where you sit will help you to diagnose how to use the book and what your particular journey is. It also explains why sometimes your boss does or says exactly the wrong thing – they don't necessarily mean to – they just don't know where on the spectrum you sit.

So, for instance, let's imagine that you place yourself as

a woman firmly in the middle of the spectrum. You've spent most of your childhood being called a tomboy. You expect to be treated in a gender-neutral way at the very least. But your alpha-male boss – who places himself at 10 on the spectrum (maybe even at 11) – sees you as a 1 or a 2: i.e., very feminine (maybe purely because he's looked at you and you're wearing a dress). This frames his expectations of you inaccurately and primes him for a less than appropriate reaction to your response. It's no wonder if there's a misunderstanding in communication that he would be less likely to encounter with another man, where the rules are simpler for him to understand. Or you might classify yourself at 2 and he wants to treat you as if you're a 6 – with the kind of banter, locker-room teasing and challenge that he might a less alpha man. And it's exactly the wrong way to speak to you, to nurture your talent, to grow your capabilities. If you're a 3 and your female boss is an 8, then you're both going to have your expectations dashed. Man or woman, we need to shed some light on the encounters we have daily, to help to navigate the gender politics that are, in some companies, crippling the business by denying talented people the opportunities to develop that they need and deserve.

At the end of our book we'll ask you to take the survey again to see if you feel you've changed, we'll reveal our choices and what they say about each of us, and our unique research, which asks the same question of a panel of business people in the UK, the USA and Russia and points to some significant trends about gender and ambition, barriers to career progression and dissatisfaction with their choice of job.

Sue Unerman and Kathryn Jacob
September, 2016

HOW TO READ THIS BOOK

ON THE WAY UP

Answer these questions and head for the chapter that resonates most

Do you worry that you're getting less than your fair share?

Do you help others without knowing what (if anything) is in it for you?

KARMA p.196

CREATIVITY p.48

Do you worry what people think of you?

Do you get called 'creative'?

Do you take the steps you should to progress your career?

Do you see others push for promotion more often than you do?

AMBITION p.16

ANGER p.173

Do you get very angry at work?

Do you never get angry at work?

Are you sometimes passed over?

Do other people get noticed more than you?

CUTTING THROUGH p.75

RESILIENCE p.142

Do you feel like giving up?

Do you take things personally?

Are there some problem relationships at work?

Do you know how to back down?

TROUBLE p.108

FROM THE TOP

Answer these questions and head for the chapter that resonates most

Do you ever break the rules for the team?

Do you see managers be unfair because it is easier and simpler?

KARMA p.196

CREATIVITY p.48

Does your team take enough appropriate risk?

Do individuals have your encouragement to disagree with the consensus?

Do women ask for promotion to an equal extent to men?

Is there an equal gender split in your senior team?

AMBITION p.16

ANGER p.173

Do you get very angry at work?

Does your team get frustrated with each other and with you?

Does everyone in your team speak up?

Have you noticed hard working team members who don't get any credit?

CUTTING THROUGH p.75

RESILIENCE p.142

Are the women in your team as resilient as they need to be?

Does your team take accountability?

Does a boy-sy locker room atmosphere dominate?

Are the team undermining each other?

TROUBLE p.108

INTRODUCTION
THE WAY FORWARD

Do you have the career you want?

Have you achieved all of your ambitions? When you look at the senior management in your company, are there as many women at the top as there are men? And the very top job, is it usually held by a woman?

It would be no surprise if you answered no to at least one of these questions. It wouldn't be a surprise at all if the answer to all of these questions was no.

A major report into the proportion of women on boards was published in late 2015. The Davies Report examined the approach to increase representation of women on boards in the UK and around the world. The UK is doing better than it used to. Appointments of women at board level to FTSE 100 companies have reached a new high at over a quarter: now 26 per cent are women. Look down a level, and the FTSE 250 has a proportion of just under 20 per cent. The report's author, Lord Davies, a former banker in his sixties, is delighted at this progress. New targets are being set for a third of directors to be women by 2020.

The last time we looked women made up more than 50 per cent of the population.

The proportion of women on boards is evidently rising.

Yet most of the women on boards in the statistics are in non-executive, part-time positions. There are only 26 executive women directors on FTSE 100 boards – that's just 9.6 per cent.

This does not indicate a pipeline for executive women on boards. Nor does it show that there is a level playing field for women to get promoted, and to achieve the careers that they deserve.

Women in work in the UK – and there are 14.5 million of them – are still not getting the same opportunities to reach the top as men.

Outside the UK, the Davies Report shows a similar picture. Norway, where a quota system has been adopted, has the most women on boards, at 35 per cent. Denmark and Germany have just over one-fifth. Then numbers dwindle. The USA has 16.9 per cent, Australia 16.2 per cent, Ireland 12.7 per cent and India 12.1 per cent.

Again, let us remind ourselves, in countries where women have always made up at least half of the population.

Not everyone in work wants to be managing director or CEO. And not every woman wants to be managing director, CEO or in any senior role. But if they do want to, then they should have the same chance to do so as men. With such large proportions of women in the workforce overall, so many millions, it is really difficult to believe that so many of them lack the ambition or ability to reach senior levels of management.

Women are not a minority in any respect, apart from in the boardroom. What is really going on, and, more to the point, what can we do about it?

We wrote this book because there is a secret that no one wants to admit.

Thousands of words have been written, numerous courses have been run.

In workplaces across the world the recurring questions of 'Why did that happen?', 'Is it just me?' and 'Does that seem fair?' play in the minds of women of all ages and roles.

The fact is that there isn't any fairness in the way that the workplace functions for women, and this book contains tips, tactics and strategies that will help you get the career you deserve. Not necessarily to get you to the top of organisations – because lots of women don't see that as the path they want to follow. This book is aimed at getting you a career that you enjoy, with the seniority you deserve, and in which your contribution is recognised.

We also know that there are men in the workplace who want the tools to make this contribution possible. They see the talent pool around them, and they see the individuals that can help the organisation thrive. Their difficulty is in being able to understand what is going on and how they can contribute to making it better, and in ensuring that they are part of making long-lasting changes that create permanent shifts in the workplace.

The workplace isn't the only part of society where women have failed to play a full part. In the UK, women have been able to stand for Parliament since 1918. It was only in 1997 that the number of female MPs reached double figures. To date there have only ever, in total, been 450 women MPs, a figure below the number of men elected in 2015 alone (459). Worldwide, there are only forty-four countries where the representation of women stands at 30 per cent or more. In Germany, a country led by one of the world's most powerful women, the percentage of female representation is 31 per cent.

So it isn't just your problem.

When we began our careers, in the 1980s, there was a good deal of talk about the glass ceiling and the fact that it was now shattered. There was a woman prime minister in the UK.

Equality for women in the workforce was a legal fact, ever since the gender equality act in 1970. There were a few women bosses around, and there were sure to be more of them as they came through the system.

Although most bosses were middle-aged men in suits, it was clear that the future for women bosses was bright. A new dawn was on the way, a future where you would expect half of the management of every company to be women, and that every other CEO would occasionally wear a skirt to work.

Three decades later, there really hasn't been very much change. Despite developments in social norms and legislation around gender discrimination, better conditions for working mothers and increased access to higher education for women in a broader range of subjects, there is no radical change in the make-up of who is running most businesses, especially at an executive full-time level. It is still men. There may be some women around board tables, but most companies continue to be predominantly managed by men.

There are more and more women in the workforce. At entry level women are doing well now, making up half or more of many industries' workforces, and this looks set to increase as women are graduating, on average, at a higher level than men. Yet year after year the statistics show that the vast majority of senior executive management are men.

Does this gender imbalance matter?

Well, it should matter – and to business in general, as well as to the women concerned. Statistics show that while tokenism (i.e., just employing one or two senior women) doesn't work, companies who have several women in senior management improve their profitability and overall performance. More women on the board means improved returns.

In research published by the *Financial Times* from the 2013 annual report of the Swedish Corporate Governance Board, Karin Thorburn – who has also taught at Dartmouth College's Tuck School of Business – says several studies show there is a positive relationship between the proportion of female board members and sales growth: 'A board does itself a disservice by being too homogeneous.' While company profitability cannot be guaranteed by merely adding more women on boards, Professor Thorburn provides examples from Australia, Spain, Singapore and Israel that show this action leads to improved company performance, such as increased shareholder value, more MBA graduates on boards, better attendance at meetings and more diverse skill sets, with board members actively seeking more information and taking an initiative. Furthermore the study indicates that firms perform better with a higher fraction of female board members, and indeed US evidence suggests that gender-balanced boards may be more efficient monitors of the CEO. A look at the Australian stock market's reaction to new outside directors shows that investors value the appointment of new female directors more than that of male directors. The stock price reaction is significantly higher (approximately 2 per cent) on the announcement of a woman. Similar results exist for Spain and Singapore.

Another paper from the research organisation Catalyst shows that firms with three or more female directors had a better profit margin than the average company by more than 40 per cent. Even a more cautious study in 2013 by Thomson Reuters, 'Mining the Metrics of Board Diversity', shows that, on average, companies with mixed-gender boards have marginally better performance when compared with a benchmark index, and less volatility in their financial results. In addition, analysis carried out across sectors also shows that companies with mixed boards have lower tracking of errors. The authors, André Chanavat and Katharine Ramsden, point to a potential competitive advantage in mixed-gender boards versus alpha-male homogeneity asking, 'Might greater gender diversity increase the performance gap between companies that do versus ones that do not?'

McKinsey Global Institute's 2015 report 'The Power of Parity' states: 'Gender inequality is not only a pressing moral and social issue but also a critical economic challenge. If women – who account for half the world's working-age population – do not achieve their full economic potential, the global economy will suffer.' They have worked out the upside of equality. In total, if every country just matches the rate of improvement of the fastest-improving country in their region, this could add as much as $12 trillion to the global economy by 2025. If every country achieved gender equality by 2025, this would rise to $28 trillion.

Too many businesses are still losing a pipeline of talented women. Solving this properly matters to the bottom line.

Do women want to reach the top?

A McKinsey report from 2012, 'Unlocking the Full Potential of Women at Work', concludes that 'Helping talented women develop and advance promises significant economic benefit to companies.' However, it also adds: 'But too many women don't want to reach the top [...] only 41% of the 200 success-ful women we interviewed declared an aspiration to join the C-suite.'

Do women really not want to reach the top? Since we're talking about half of this country's population, surely even if a smaller proportion of women than men have such ambitions, there are still enough women aiming for the top. Are women conflicted about the work/life balance when they have children? Yes, of course. But, as this book will show, this is an issue that can be examined and addressed. Our own experiences prove that it's not an insurmountable barrier, and that it's possible to start a family while maintaining a high-level career.

Indeed, KPMG's 2014 report 'Cracking the Code' included statistics showing that women with children are more likely to have received five or more promotions than women without children – although both groups of women were much less likely to have been promoted than men in equivalent positions.

It is clear to us that with even a 1 per cent advantage for business resulting from a more balanced senior management team – and the vast majority of evidence suggests that there's far more to gain than that – companies must rise to the challenge of promoting their valuable women employees, and of not losing them if they become new mums.

Our interviews for this book show that far too few companies take this view, hiding behind inappropriate notions of 'level playing fields' at what must be considerable long-term value and cultural loss.

Remember, the glass ceiling was supposedly shattered over forty years ago. Legislation ensured that it was dismantled. Worldwide the law varies, although most countries now, at least, penalise or prevent the dismissal of pregnant women. Still not every country mandates equal pay for equal work. Across the EU maternity leave is diverse, ranging from twelve weeks to fifty-eight weeks, and paternity leave varies massively. The detail of legal gender equality varies from Australia to Austria and beyond. The truth is clear in most countries. Even where the legal glass ceiling is gone, most women at work, at one time or another, will come up against a block to their careers that men with a similar level of talent know how to overcome. Do men know something, then, that women don't?

Yes actually they do. We will explain and decode it in these pages.

Every woman is entitled to achieve her full potential at work and, at the same time, a good work/life balance. There are millions at the moment who are not.

**Even where there is no glass ceiling …
there is instead a glass divide, a glass wall.**

You can see through it, to the meetings that you're excluded from or the casual conversations that accelerate careers that you aren't participating in. Men and women can see each other very clearly through the glass, but they don't speak the same language or have equivalent cultural expectations. For some women a glass wall appears where there has been nothing there before because of a change of management or role. One of our interviewees described the challenge that came about when she got a new boss. Although he had lived in America, her home country, for over a decade, and was to all intents and purposes an American, she discovered that he'd been brought up in a society in another part of the world, where he had formed an expectation for a level of deference from women in general that she had never experienced. Once she got over her surprise and dismay, we find how she dealt with this in the book. For other women it is so customary, so habitual, to be the wrong side of a glass wall that they don't even try to break through.

The glass wall has several aspects. Some are to do with the culture of the company you're working in: it might not have a tradition of senior women, or it might be just too homogeneous (for example, the board are all white middle-aged men in suits) to allow outliers (and being a women might make you an outlier in this respect) to progress. There are walls built from managers' nervousness around maternity leave (whatever the official company policy) or inability to understand that not everyone laughs at the same jokes or behaves as if they're in a boys' locker room.

Then there are the walls that result from how women are brought up, really from our culture. The way we are expected to behave by schools, by our friends, perhaps by our parents. These walls block women and not men; men just don't have these walls in the same way. (They may experience other ones, built from society's expectations from them, but that is another book, not this one.) If you haven't spotted the wall yet or don't know where the wall comes from, you will have trouble getting rid of it, so this is the time to be very clear about it.

The glass walls that come about from cultural expectations are deep-rooted and have lasted for a very long time. The US career consultant Janice Larouche, writing back in the 1980s, described the tendency for some women to come up against blocks that are derived from a notion of femininity that's deep-rooted in most cultures. This, then, is where some of the walls come from, and because our cultures change at a very slow pace, the issues she mentioned back then are still around, even if the strategies, language and tactics to deal with them must be updated and made contemporary.

As part of the background to the book, we commissioned research across three countries to assess what men and women felt about their careers. The majority of those surveyed in the UK, Russia and the USA felt that women encountered barriers to their careers. So we know there is an issue and we've recognised it. No secret there. There's more about this illuminating Lightspeed research in the appendix at the back of the book. A clear finding is that a greater percentage of men than women say that they are very ambitious. It seems that women are ambiguous about the word 'ambition'. It feels strident and harsh, at odds with our sense of self as women. Societally, does that indicate that we see ambition as the preserve of men? Is there a glass wall in the fact that females are unwilling to articulate their ambition so that career fulfilment is unattainable?

Within the pages that follow you will find advice that doesn't require you, as a woman, to become a 'man' in order to thrive at work. There is another way that enables you to stay true to your sense of self and not be forced into the roles that make you uncomfortable. You will find challenging advice as you follow your path through the book, but none of it will require you to role-play for the rest of your career.

This ambivalence around ambition is one of the most common glass walls in the office. Women can be less single-minded than men sometimes about what they might have to sacrifice for the next promotion. Rather than this being a reason for standing still or moving sideways, it could be that women just need helping through that version of the glass wall. That does not make them less able for a senior role: in fact, it might even make them better at it, as they seek improvements in how things are run beyond the pursuit of power and status.

If acknowledging your ambition is your glass wall, we're providing detailed advice of how to get past it here.

Being too open is another aspect of the glass wall. Often young women enter the workplace wanting to be true to themselves, and to stay in touch with their feelings. This authenticity is absolutely crucial to a great career, but so is knowing when to deploy it and when to disguise it. You have to be aware that every word you say in any workplace setting (including the bar across the road) is taken literally and might get used against you. Sometimes you need to be measured in how you react in the moment.

It should be enough to be very good at the task elements of the job, shouldn't it? Well, yes and no. Another common glass wall for women is believing that getting work done as efficiently as possible is enough to build a career. Getting stuff done is an incredible asset professionally. It is not enough, however. You will not get promoted to a senior management position *solely* because you are highly efficient.

There's the putting-yourself-down glass wall. Women are often quick to take the blame for something going wrong, and famously tend to recite their flaws rather than their talents. If you are negative about yourself in the wrong context, however attractively modest this may seem, then your detractors will repeat it and use it against you.

There are many more aspects of the glass wall detailed in these pages: perfectionism – time-consuming self-editing, which is ultimately self-defeating when others are being promoted for a good enough job done; the work/family delusion – your boss is not your dad, your team are not your siblings (or your kids); desire for security – settling for a safe, more junior role instead of shooting for the stars; needing to be liked – never wanting to have to make an unpopular call; not wanting to fight – being compliant is not what you get paid for in a senior role.

Is it right or fair that this should hold women back? Maybe not. But that does not change a thing. What women need is to see the glass wall when they come up against it, to know what to do about it, and to go against some of what society expects in order to break through the wall and then make a difference to how business currently operates. More women in senior positions will change workplace culture.

This book gives you practical techniques to smash the glass walls and to take the senior position that you have earned.

This book contains the advice that no one ever gives you in training sessions or coaching. It's practical and applicable, and the advice works.

In the chapters that follow we'll explain our strategies for success, and ways to avoid the pitfalls of failure. Our purpose is not only to arm women with strategies to help them stay on their desired career path, but also to open up and explain the mainly hidden gender politics that are in operation. We will reveal the glass walls and show you what to do about them to make real changes to the current, highly unsatisfactory, status quo.

The case studies you will read are all based on fact (although most identities are disguised at the request of many of our interviewees). Many will be shared experiences, things perhaps that you have gone through where you have felt alone in a situation that in fact is common to many of us. If you take the advice and try the strategies out, you will find that they will change things at work. The advice is practical and, while sometimes counter-intuitive or even against what is thought of as common wisdom, it is tried and tested and it will work. What you will read may sometimes surprise you. It may even shock you. But that is what is needed now. The glass wall will not disappear by itself. It has been standing there, blocking the progress of women at work for decades. Together we need to take it down, and that will not happen if we are too earnest or euphemistic. We need to face up to the situation and make real change happen.

Our opening chapter concerns ambition. Time and time again, as discussed, it appears that where men are openly ambitious, women are ambivalent, not sure if a senior position will suit them. Unclear whether they want to behave in the way that they think they need to in order to achieve their goals at work. Well, sometimes you need to steel yourself to do so, but sometimes you don't. We will show how you can be yourself by being clear about what you want and what you don't want. How you can change any role to suit your own personal style.

Another common theme is that men show off their **creativity** in a way that many women do not. **Men strut their stuff. Women end up feeling that they must conform at work in order to get on. The second chapter deals with this issue,** and if you worry about what people think about you at work, or if anyone has ever said that you are not creative, then these strategies will help you progress.

Chapter 3 concerns cutting through in the workplace. Men like to be noticed, women like to get on with the work. If you have ever felt too busy getting on with your work to spend time promoting yourself, then you need to re-evaluate because you will be passed over. This chapter shows you what to do and how to reverse this situation.

Sometimes things just really do go badly wrong at work. For everyone or anyone. It really is not the end of the world, but it does often feel as though trouble troubles women in a completely different way from how it troubles men. There are very different pitfalls and very, very different consequences. **Chapter 4 takes a frank and unexpurgated look at what can go wrong and what to do about it if it does.**

Men take things in their stride that knock women out. **Chapter 5 examines the importance of persistence, flexibility and industry**. You can learn **resilience**. If you are knocked down, get back up again; you can do it, and you will succeed.

Do you ever get angry at work – so angry that you don't know how to deal with it? Or do you never ever get angry? Culturally men are expected to exploit their inner bastard, while women are expected to hide their fury and just get on with things. **Anger is an energy. Don't fight it, use it. Chapter 6 shows you how.**

We end with a chapter devoted to Karma, to paying favours forward and to making up for the fact that women's networks differ from those of men. Women are not in the network of chaps. Here's how to generate Karma in the workplace. How helping others helps you.

One of the intentions of this book is to make it clear that no woman is alone in what she is going through.

There is strength in understanding shared experiences. Interspersed throughout the book are extended extracts from our interviews with individuals who are at a true turning point in their working lives. This is unedited, presented anonymously so that the interviewees could expose their true feelings to us, uninhibited by conventional manners or self-restraint. We will hear from Tessa, who is taking a career break because her work/life balance is out of kilter; from Kelly, a single mum in full-time work whose employers are really keen to make sure that she gets no extra help (well, it would be so unfair to everyone else, wouldn't it?); from Mercedes, in a top City job, considering the next stage of her career; from Rachel, who is about to return to work from her second maternity leave; from Megan, whose first job after graduating has not lived up to expectations; from Gloria, who is considering retirement after forty years of work; and from Carys, who has built her career through a combination of straight talking and charm. We don't know yet what the choices these individuals were making at the time of talking to us will mean in their lives. But we believe that you, like us, will be touched and inspired by their honesty and the questions they are asking themselves. Perhaps some of their stories will provide a comfort or an inspiration, knowing that others are going through similar experiences to your own.

There are forty-one strategies detailed in the chapters that follow. They cover a range of situations that include:

- How to ask for a promotion and what to do when you hear the word 'no';
- What to do when you've done something that should have stayed private but everyone is talking about you;
- Picking your fights: when and how to use your anger;
- How to break the rules of the office to your advantage;
- Getting your point across by changing the language to speak theirs;
- How to be seen (even if you're not a show-off);
- What to do when it feels like no one is on your side, or it feels like you're drowning;
- How to say 'no' when your work/life boundaries are being challenged by work and still get promoted;
- How to negotiate a level playing field – in fact, more than level, one that favours you.

We have a mission. It's time to take down the glass wall. Let's go.

CHAPTER 1

AMBITION

....

Men are ambitious; women are ambivalent

During your career you're sure to be asked a number of questions. Some of them you can answer unequivocally; others are more nuanced. One of the trickiest questions is when you're asked 'Are you ambitious?' That's because ambition has a different meaning for every individual.

To some people 'Are you ambitious?' implies that you're a no-holds-barred, fight-to-the-death, trample-on-colleagues kind of person who is never satisfied until they have an office the size of a football pitch, two executive assistants and a seat on the corporate jet. To answer 'I am ambitious but …' seems limp and self-serving. The fact is that you can be ambitious without it making you a version of yourself that you don't like.

Cilla Snowball CBE, who heads up AMV BBDO, a leading advertising agency, has achieved a huge amount in her working life. She describes being interviewed by a journalist who asked her if she was ambitious. Cilla responded by saying that she was ambitious for her colleagues and her clients. This remark seemed completely incongruous to the reporter, who implied that she wasn't being entirely truthful: surely no one could hit the highest levels in advertising without having a driving personal ambition? Wasn't that a typical 'advertising' response, laced with spin? The simple truth is that, unless everyone who works with Cilla shares the same ambition as her, the company doesn't have momentum and a forward-looking view. Similarly, clients doing well shows that the partnership is working for them and they challenge AMV to do more. It's a mutual growth rather than an individual one.

From the earliest stage of childhood girls play together. It's a consensual type of play about building allegiances and sharing. Boys play rough-and-tumble games, shoot each other and then get up and do it again. Not many people 'die' during an intense playground game at school, but boys learn it's them against the others and that, if you get shot down, you live to fight again. This is one interesting view on how early team-building and resilience and ambition are learned, documented in academic research: for example, 'When Boys and Girls Play', from 2007, by J. G. Riley and R. B. Jones, which examined the gender differences in play among children and its implications. It also explains some behaviour in meetings that we've both experienced.

'Are you ambitious?'

If it is one of the trickiest questions, it is also one of the most interesting ones. Increasingly we need to be equipped to answer, 'Yes, on my terms', without it framing expectations of the individual not wanting to progress. If you have children under the age of six, a job where you are unable to balance their needs and yours can create an untenable situation. It may sound glamorous to have a job that enables you to work globally, but the reality can be that every Monday morning you get up at 4 a.m. to get to the airport in time to fly for three hours, sit in a room and fly home in time to get in after 9 p.m. One interviewee said that after a while they only knew where they were by the colour of the taxis. They weren't at home, they had minimal impact on the places they visited and the idea of getting on a plane to go on holiday had no appeal.

Ask yourself the question – could I get broader experience in a sideways move that might serve me better in the long term? Careers aren't always about linear progression; they can be about becoming the generalist who can look in more places for challenges.

Throughout the course of this chapter we will look at a number of women and how they responded to the challenge of ambition. We begin with Deidre, who has more ambition than she knows what to do with.

Ask for what you want; ask for what you need

Deidre feels lost in her new job. It sounded brilliant when she took it. She was to be in charge of a new, dedicated strategy team. She was going in a little bit over her head, of course. At her old firm she had always been congratulated for her grasp of strategy and won internal awards for her work, but she had been part of a team. With this new role she is completely out of her comfort zone. Her best friend had said to her, 'Your life starts where your comfort zone ends.' She had bought several new outfits during her week off work so that she could completely reinvent herself. She'd developed a mini-crush on her new boss. And after her first few weeks she's completely miserable, she isn't sleeping properly and she feels like she is letting her new boss down badly.

The problem in a nutshell is that she has no idea how to go about managing the situation. She knows exactly how to do good work herself. She is now in charge of six people, and clearly the task of getting them to do good work requires a completely different skill set. Her boss, who really likes her, has his own problems, however. He has made the move to appoint a new strategy team because of the success of one of their competitors – the company that he in fact poached Deidre from. But he doesn't know how she should do her job either, as strategy is something that he has never cared about very much. He has acted impulsively and has given Deidre a huge pay packet and told her to get on with it. That he has every faith in her. But, despite his assurances, his door is not always open. He has lots of other direct reports to deal with. Many of whom resent the newcomer to the senior management team, so they are not exactly being helpful. Also Deidre is the only woman among them.

What's going through Deidre's head? She is thinking, 'He hates me because I am letting him down. I'm rubbish. I'm awful.'

Deidre's main problem here is that she is taking everything personally. She believed the hype when offered the job. She built up the idea that only she could deliver in this new role. She knew it was tough, but she had no idea how tough. She should have gone to someone outside the business for advice. First, in not taking it personally. Second, in asking for the help she needs. She should now be thinking, 'Do I want this job anyway? It is not what I expected, and I could not have known what it would be like here. But if I do want this job, how can my boss help me?'

Doing a good job is never all about you – especially when you lead a team, of course. Deidre had never had leadership training. She should have asked for it. She had never liaised with HR before, and she should have done that too.

Deidre was unable to look at the situation with perspective. Of course, her boss wanted her to succeed. He'd promoted her into the role. But he had no idea what she needed. She had to ask for it. And her idea that she was failing because she could not do everything herself is part of the superwoman myth that stalks women at work. It is not all high-flying success or being rubbish. There is a spectrum in between. This 'all or nothing' approach doesn't surprise us. It is not uncommon. Deidre has succeeded in her career up until this new role by working on her own. She has no experience of real teamwork. Like many girls, she gave up on team sports at school when she became a teenager (other things to worry about), and the school pretty much gave up on making her participate.

There's a key difference in many education experiences between the genders. From the tendency to be involved in more active play from a very young age, boys then do continue to participate in sport at school, and many, if not most, follow a team all through their lives. Even if they aren't sporty. Worldwide over two-thirds of men follow sport, in contrast to just over 40 per cent of women. At school many girls opt out, and are allowed to. Their out-of-work interests do not revolve around sport in the same way. Could this mean that they grow up without the same level of instinctive under-standing of teams, despite the fact that they are stereotypically judged to be more collaborative? In their publication *From Elite Female Athletes to Exceptional Leaders* the professional services firm Ernst and Young show research that indicates a direct correlation between girls' participation in sport and greater achievement in higher education and employment – in fact, they say 'a majority of leading female executives first found success in athletics'.

If you don't love sport, can you succeed in your career?

And if you are meant to be collaborative, can you be ambitious, or is that unfeminine?

Let's be very clear here. Ambition is not taboo for women.

If you want a promotion, ask for it. Women are notorious for ruling themselves out of senior positions because they consider themselves unqualified. A few years ago Hewlett-Packard ran an investigation into why more women weren't in top management positions. They concluded: 'Women working at HP applied for a promotion only when they believed they met 100 per cent of the qualifications listed for the job. Men were happy to apply when they thought they could meet 60 per cent of the job requirements.' One global talent manager has told us that in five years of interviewing for over forty CEO jobs worldwide she has only seen five female candidates. That women in her view just don't reach for the top jobs. Equally, however, the next top job may not be the one for you. Don't automatically take the roles that you are offered. Work out your strengths and your weaknesses, and look for a career path that plays to your strengths. You do not have to be super-woman. You don't have to be an elite athlete. Frankly, Deidre has taken the wrong job this time round, but, having landed herself in a situation, she needed to get support to get herself out of it. Remember that your boss has a vested interest in your success. He will want you to succeed, but is not a mind-reader and will not know what you need. Ask for the job you want. Ask for the help you need. Be clear, and don't take any setbacks personally. It will not help.

AMBITION STRATEGY 1

Ask for what you want; ask for what you need

On the way up

Not everyone suits the next job up. When you start your career, you are usually given a role where you are needed by the business. Hopefully that works out, and you are offered the next role up. At some point you need to take stock, ask yourself what job it is that you want next, that you ultimately want, and start planning to get it. The simplest way is to ask for it. But when you do, make sure that you get all the support you need – training, mentoring, support from your peers. Business is a team game.

From the top

Beware the Peter Principle. It is all too easy to assume that someone's performance when promoted is going to equate to their success in the previous more junior role. It may not. Particularly without careful understanding of what training and support they need. Do not assume that your candidate will know what they need, or how to ask for it.

CASE STUDY 2

Ambition is a stranger to me

It's a beautiful spring day in a proper bluebell wood. The fifth annual Easter egg hunt is under way. There are three families, with nine children between them – eight girls and one boy. He's just turned three, and it is really the first time he has been properly involved. He's the youngest of all, but only by a few moments, as he's a twin.

As it is the fifth time these three families have got together, the ritual of the egg hunt is well established. Dads go out and hide mini eggs and miniature golden bunnies in the woods, careful to stay near the path, avoiding brambles and any incitement to trample the stunning bluebell display. Then the oldest girls, aged twelve, usher the smaller kids around, collecting up all the eggs. Back to the grown-ups to pool the spoils and share them out equally. So far so good, so far so according to tradition. Until Peter, the youngest, charges back to the picnic site and loudly announces, 'I've won!!' 'Won?' Won what? It isn't a competition. Until this year. Up until this year the girls have collected eggs and shared them out. Peter was a bit too small to know exactly what was going on. This year Peter has found a golden mini bunny and has decided, apparently off his own bat, that this means that he's beaten everyone else.

His dad says, beaming: 'Yes Peter, you have won.' The rest of the grown-ups (well, particularly the other mothers, mothers of girls) were astonished that this amicable little ritual had turned into a contest where the boy won and therefore implicitly all the girls had lost.

How bred in the bone is this ambition to beat the rest of them? Is it a masculine trait?

Peter's mother, Jane, happens to be near the top of her profession and runs a large team. Her career has been on hold while the kids were small, but she now has the energy and time to put back into climbing the career ladder. She is the first to acknowledge, however, that she doesn't push herself, and that she has time and again been in the situation where she could have shown off her achievements but has instead stayed in the background. Jane says: 'You do have opportunities, you do have the ability to succeed. But if you bump into your boss, and he's aware that you're in the middle of tackling a situation, and he says to you, "How's it going?", you will say back to him, "Oh it's fine, I'm handling it." A man in the same situation will talk specifics at length. He will say, "It's fine, I have done this, I have made this happen, I have saved the day." He will draw attention to himself.'

She goes on: 'In my company there are annual excellence awards. You can apply every year, there are financial gains, there are promotions. It is up to you to represent the extra things you've done outside of your day job – for example, raising issues about safety in the workplace or customer care. I know men who have a very large number of these awards. I know many women who will say, "I haven't done anything worthy this year so I won't bother." They're just happier with less publicity and in fact with less reward – at least, some of them. It seems more important for the men to promote themselves. They have an inbuilt belief that they have a right to do it. It is important to them to have senior management recognition. I'll think, "I've had a good day, now I've got to go home, I've got stuff to do." The awards are just not as crucial to me.'

She doesn't think that her ambivalence to ambition is bred in the bone because of her gender. She says of her youngest child, Peter: 'That boy thing, that competitiveness, it's the male role models around him.'

Academic studies endorse the view that the self-promotion drive in men is a result of learned behaviour. The psychiatrist Anna Fels writes, in *Harvard Business Review*, on the question of whether women lack ambition, that in childhood ambitions for both genders two elements join together: mastery of a skill and recognition. She says:

> looking through studies on the development of boys and girls, I noticed that they virtually always identified the same two components of childhood ambition. There was a plan that involved a real accomplishment requiring work and skill, and there was an expectation of approval in the form of fame, status, acclaim, praise or honour.

Yet grown women have a tendency to 'refuse to claim a central, purposeful place in their own stories, eagerly shifting the credit elsewhere and shunning recognition'. Fels argues strongly that this shift comes about because society from pre-school onwards denies equivalent recognition to girls, especially when they are in competition for it from boys. In a study she cites of nursery school, 'all of the teachers gave more attention to boys … they got both more physical and verbal rewards. Boys also received more direction from the teachers and were twice as likely as the girls to get individual instruction.'

Of course, as a woman who is dedicated to her career, to doing a good job and to raising her family, Jane is a busy woman. So her priorities are split between work and home. But in addition to having strong boundaries of time set by childcare needs, there is another factor that she acknowledges. At work she balances what she'd like to achieve for herself with a huge satisfaction in improving what her company can do. 'My male peers might say, "I'm done here, I've achieved everything I can here and it's time for me to move on." I don't feel like that at all. I get real satisfaction from the business improving. From knowing that I am making a difference to all our clients, to all the people I work with.'

It is not uncommon for women to be more identified with the company that they work for, so that their ambition for themselves is sublimated into an ambition for everyone that works there. It feels very, very common for women to be less interested in self-promotion than in doing a good job. Of course, it is not impossible for women to be both like Jane and like Jane's son Peter, for women to care about the business overall *and* also to be personally competitive.

AMBITION STRATEGY 2

Ambition is a stranger to me

On the way up

Look at how the men around you behave. Don't let yourself

be left behind because they self-promote more aggressively than you do. You don't have to spend all day blowing your own trumpet (you're probably too busy), but you should take the time at least every month to let your boss know what you you've done that is particularly good. If you don't tell them, how on earth will they know?

From the top

Make sure that you encourage the women in your team to have a structured opportunity every month to tell you what they've achieved. Don't make it gruelling. Don't let it become an ordeal. Ask open questions about what they're most proud of, tease it out of them and then make sure that you repeat back to them what you think it is that they've excelled at.

Now we move on to Erin, who has never for one moment doubted that she would do whatever it takes to get on.

You may well find that this story challenges the boundaries of what you think is acceptable behaviour in the office. Our publisher really wasn't sure that it should be included. But we would ask you whether you would react as strongly if the story was about what a man did to get his ambitions achieved as you may be as it stands here, and as it was recounted to us. Perhaps you would judge that this is not acceptable behaviour from anyone; or perhaps it seems worse because it seems in some way *'unfeminine'*. Either way Erin, who has achieved everything she set out to do in her subsequent career, felt that at the time, in a very *masculine*-orientated business environment, she had no choice if she wanted to progress.

CASE STUDY 3

Jostling the big boys

Erin is one of the only women in her field. She wanted to be in politics, but instead found herself simply randomly applying for jobs when her time at university ended, purely to make ends meet. The job she took was simply the first one she was offered at a decent salary. Her heart was still set on finding a way into Westminster.

A moment came when she accepted that this really seemed like it was not to be. Were her views too extreme? (Surely not.) Was she too pushy? (Is that even possible in that field?)

Gradually, almost imperceptibly, her ambition began to shift in focus to her current role. Partly because of Geoffrey. Geoffrey is the next most senior person in her office. Her immediate boss. He's talented, he's good-looking. He has effortless charm. He's completely at home in the boys' club atmosphere of their business. She can see all that, but she can also see two other things. First, that if she waits for him to get promoted before she gets his job, she'll be waiting a long time – he just doesn't seem to be in a hurry to move up. Second, that if she chooses to believe that he will eventually suggest that she is promoted to his level, she will be waiting even longer. It is not that he doesn't recognise her skills, even though what she is good at is not the same as what he is good at – for a start, he can be patient and she can't. It's that the business has a strictly linear management structure, and it is obvious that there is no appetite to change what is working. There is a number one, a department chief (mainly does client lunches and the golf course), and a number two (Geoffrey, who organises the work) and then a set of group heads who report into him (who get the work done and who include Erin).

Would most of us do what Erin does next? In a field with very few senior women, the chances are that her choice is to fight her way to the top or to leave. At the time in question she feels that she has no choice because her only other career option (climbing the political ladder) isn't going to happen.

She says about her next step: 'Well I suppose I was quite devious.' Judge for yourself. Not many of us would feel comfortable with what she did.

Erin waits for Geoffrey's next annual leave. She then goes to their boss, Adrian, and suggests that, while Geoffrey is away, she should take over his biggest account. She says: 'I met the client recently and we absolutely got on like a house on fire. You know he has never really warmed to Geoff – not really. I absolutely think that I can win him over.'

It is a pack of lies. Erin has never met the client. Geoffrey has a great relationship with him. Unfortunately for Geoffrey, whose career trajectory never actually recovers from this, he is away for three weeks in Australia with his family. Erin takes on the account, delivers some first-class client service and, when Geoffrey comes back from holiday and demands the account back, tells him to 'f**k off'.

By the autumn Erin is at an equal level with Geoffrey, she has better accounts, and in the long run she has much better career prospects. Roll on a few years, and Geoffrey is no longer in the industry.

Erin works in a macho, testosterone-driven sector. On that scale of 1 to 10 (where 1 is very feminine and 10 is very masculine) Erin would score herself a feminine 4. She could easily have been overlooked if she'd played by the rules, and she did establish a great client relationship that benefited the business. Should she have lied? Was there another way?

Jostling the big boys

On the way up

If you feel that your career path is blocked, if you feel that things aren't fair or aren't moving quickly enough, then you're entitled to break the rules. Don't outright lie, though. Most of the time you'll get caught out – there are few of us with the absolute chutzpah to carry this one off.

From the top

You have to be able to spot talent, even if it comes in an unconventional form. There are still business sectors, where in a way, women have to pretend to be like men – constantly dressing in black and white, speaking in carefully modulated low tones – before they gradually, eventually, painfully get considered for a promotion. Wake up to talent, whatever form it takes. Keep an eye out for managers that are milking the performance of talented members of their team, whatever the gender. Are you enquiring why someone isn't being put up for promotion when they seem to be performing well? It wouldn't be the first time that an individual won't countenance losing a number two because they'd have to get more hands on with the work.

Next, Justine needed a blockage in her way before she ever thought to fight for her promotion.

Use the frustration

Justine works at a small but flourishing business in the strategic planning division. There are about forty-five employees overall. Her boss is the director of planning, and she is one of two deputies in the department. She thinks that the meeting which proved a catalyst to her career progression came about because the other deputy, Kyle, left to go to another job.

She knows that her boss, Shane, prefers Kyle to her: they play golf together and share a locker-room sense of humour that she does her best to avoid. There has been a recent gruelling Christmas outing where Shane had suggested that everyone told a joke to kick off the evening. Shane's was so offensive that she could barely get through the rest of the evening, and this had not helped to warm the relationship personally. Still, she isn't worried: she has great credentials and she is confident that her results are at the top of her field.

Kyle's resignation comes as a bit of surprise to everyone – he had not seemed restless. Shane tries to replace him but after interviewing a dozen candidates grudgingly agrees to Justine's suggestion that he promote from within the department. This was a good move for healthy growth, but it puts Shane in a very bad mood. He takes Justine to one side for a chat. 'I just want you to be clear, Justine, given that I have just promoted someone who works for you to be your equal, that there is no promotion on the cards for you.'

Justine reacts with some alarm, naturally. Shane continues: 'You see, there is only room for one director of planning in this agency, and that is me.'

There does not seem much point in answering this statement. In fact, Justine finds it so ridiculous that she is not as upset as you would think. Perhaps not as much as she should be. Shane has not made her miserable; Shane has made her motivated.

She goes for a drink with one of her friends outside the business. His career trajectory has been swift, but somewhat bumpy. He has just been promoted to run his division, but his promotion is swiftly followed by the resignation of three key colleagues because they will not report into him as their new boss. She feels sure he will have a good idea what she should do next. 'You're going to have to kill Shane, aren't you then?' he says. 'Find some way of getting him out of your way.' (She assumes he is talking metaphorically but has never actually asked.) The message she takes from this discussion is that she should ignore Shane's statement completely.

Her very next step is to seek a conversation with the man she feels closest to out of all of the men on the all-male board. They have a business trip planned, which goes well, and on the train on the way back to the office she speaks her mind and just asks him when he thinks she could become a board director at their company. Jonathan answers, 'I'm not sure Justine, but I can't see that there is any hurry – you're doing incredibly well so far.'

Justine is surprised by this. She is twenty-eight, and many of her peers have been promoted to boards of similar companies. At the last place she had worked her boss had made managing director by thirty. She says as much, giving as examples people that they both know.

'Yes,' Jonathan replies. 'Exactly – they're all men. Name me one woman you know who's near a board position at your age and with your experience.'

Justine is literally speechless for a few moments. This is not the Victorian era. Women have had the vote and equal pay and an equal right to a board position for decades and decades. She does not hesitate to set Jonathan straight. It appears that he actually thinks that gender is a factor, and she bluntly explains its complete irrelevance. Three months later Jonathan is made MD of the company. His first action as MD is to promote Justine to the board.

Use the frustration

On the way up

Justine probably would have eventually reached the promotion she wanted, but it would certainly have taken longer if Shane had not made it seem impossible. If someone puts barriers in your way, use them as a leaping-off point. Use the energy that frustration gives you to propel you towards your objective.

Tess Alps, now non-exec chair of Thinkbox, the marketing body for commercial television in the UK, thinks back to a career block that crystallised her ambition from thirty years ago. She was working at a TV company, and her boss was promoted to become its first female sales director, a move much heralded as a turning point in the industry. Tess should have been her number two, but her boss said she just couldn't be – you just couldn't have two women running the team. Despite a history of achievement, Tess had never been ambitious for power in the industry until the point at which it was denied to her because she was a woman. She used that energy to achieve a sterling career, including running two companies. While this kind of attitude is unlikely to be explicit these days, it may have just been driven underground into an unspoken prejudice. It was almost easier to deal with when it was out in the open, because it could be tackled head on. Now, a boss would never say that they would not promote someone because they were a woman. They might say: there's a lack of presence or gravitas. If you're being stalled for promotion when you're achieving hard performance criteria (e.g., meeting sales targets), then you need to get absolute specifics and ask for training to overcome any barriers.

From the top

Quite what Shane thought he was going to achieve by telling Justine she couldn't progress is a mystery: did he see her as a rival that he hoped to get to leave? Jonathan suffered from a not uncommon hidden bias. Because Justine was a woman, he assumed her career could meander. It is impressive that, when this bias was pointed out to him, he went out of his way to support her. If this kind of bias is going on in your business, then it needs to be uncovered. If fewer women are making progress than men, then, frankly, it probably means that this is the case.

Feel the fear, then do it anyway

Nina has hated every single promotion she has had, despite the fact that she has reached the top of her profession and driven the profitability of her company up by millions. Her job satisfaction now is second to none.

Nina, who is chair of the highly successful business that she helped to build and also a non-executive director of significant standing, has had to be very brave at every single stage of her career progression. She began as a secretary, she didn't go to university, and has earned every rung on the ladder through listening and learning. She's risen to the top of her field, but she didn't plan to do so. Her ambition came from watching others around her, believing that she could do the job at least as well, and hating being left out or left behind.

'I have never thought I need to work twice as hard as anyone. What I have done is be prepared to ask questions and learn from people who clearly know more about something

than me, so I have never had an ego that has got in the way ...
The one thing that I have done more than anything else is to be
quite brave. I have been stretched really far out of my comfort
zone at times, and I have gone home to my personal world
and have been very scared. On those kind of dark moments
when you do have that self-doubt which I do believe that a
lot of women have, I think you have just got to be brave. And
face up to it.'

Nina recalls one particular time when she was asked to take
over running the business's largest client. The client had been
on the point of firing the business and moving his millions
elsewhere. A lengthy renegotiation of terms and service conditions had finally saved the day, but one of those conditions
was a change of senior manager in the business. She was asked
to take it on, and the final condition of a renewed contract
was that the man in charge liked her. 'The man in charge was
tough, all I had heard about him was how tough he was. Gosh,
you go into every meeting with him and he will grill you,
challenge you, try to destroy you.'

It's true that he didn't suffer fools gladly, and in her first
meeting with him he was clearly trying to see if she was tough
enough to work with him. All the other senior executives in
the organisation had failed to turn this business critical relationship around. Losing it would mean redundancies and a
significant change in fortunes. Nina was very clear what was
at stake. She was scared, but she was also prepared. Nina takes
up the story: 'I went in to meet him and he gave me a list of
twenty things that we had done wrong. And he said, "Take me
through exactly what you're going to do to put them right." It
was one of those moments where you sink or swim. I thought:
"OK, you want the detail, I will give you the detail, but it is
not just us that has to change – you are going to have to change
as an organisation too." I spent over two hours with him one

to one. I told him what we would do, and I told him what he needed his people to do. Afterwards my boss came back in while he delivered the verdict. He said, "Yep, she'll do. I don't know how you'll manage her, but she'll get us sorted out." It was like a rite of passage for me. I thought I can go out now and deal with the rest of the world.'

She felt the same fear when her boss asked her to take over eventually as CEO. She hadn't asked for the promotion, but she did know that she deserved it and she was not going to allow her anxiety let someone else take over instead. 'I remember that the following day was the same day as my little boy was starting school. I'd taken him to school, big school, and he was pretty scared and looking to me for reassurance. I had exactly the same feeling when I walked up the road to work that day. I walked through the door, and I thought I've got to be brave. I told my little boy to be brave and I have got to be brave. It was incredibly difficult.'

Nina's growth in confidence is unusual, according to *Forbes Magazine* writer Susan Adams. More commonly women lose confidence and ambition once they get to work. Women are statistically much more ambitious than men when they first arrive at new jobs. In a 2014 Bain report 43 per cent of female new starters aspire to reach top management versus only 34 per cent of men. But just two years into their careers women's goals 'fall off a cliff'. While male ambition stays consistent at one in three, only 16 per cent of women now say they want to be top managers. If you're already speculating that this is because they're planning to look after children instead, then think again. The marriage and children statistics are the same for ambitious types as for those who lost their ambition. The reason is that they don't feel supported by their managers, and they have a hard time fitting into the stereotypes of success that they see within their business.

Nina remembers her boss helping her to navigate this very problem. 'In my first sessions in my boss's office there was a management team of four, with me as the only woman. Our boss would be looking for suggestions about how we were going to move forward, and my two male colleagues would be wading in with all these big statements. You know: we've got to do this, or we've got to do that, very aggressive in language and in direction – they implied their proposals were obvious – the only way forward. It made me feel as though I just could not challenge what they were saying because I would look stupid if I did. But my boss ensured that my voice was heard. If I said that I wasn't convinced about something and they began jeering, then he would say, "Hang on a minute, let Nina speak, let's understand what she is questioning." You do need that encouragement, and you do need to train your management team, especially the men, to operate in a different way.'

Nina had to find her way to fight her corner. Counter-intuitively, perhaps, it was behaving in exactly the opposite way to the alpha men she was partnered with. Speaking very quietly, listening, understanding when to make her point and never joining in the fracas. Although her two male equivalents never actually changed behaviour in those meetings, they did sometimes approach her separately and acknowledge her perspective and how valuable it was to have a point of view from a completely different standpoint from their own. This is one of the big benefits, of course, of diversity, just as one of the colossal mistakes that successful businesses can make is to have too many people all in the same mould, in violent agreement with each other. It may bring short-term success, but it will not give you the strength and depth to survive and adapt to changing circumstances.

Feel the fear, then do it anyway

On the way up

Feel the fear but do it anyway. Don't let nerves put you off. You have almost certainly earned the right for your promotion, pay rise or award. Just because other people shout louder than you, that does not make them better. Find a technique to give yourself courage. Nina thought of her little boy's first day at school. You might find telling yourself in the mirror in the bathroom in the morning that you are the best ever works for you. Or taking yourself to the ladies' toilet and deep breathing for a couple of minutes. Feel the fear, face the fear, then do it anyway.

From the top

Nina's boss had the insight to see her talent and encourage her to be brave. This meant taking the time to spot her talent. If you can't see the talent in the quieter people – which often means the women – then slow down, try harder, look deeper. We know of one major retail chain where the majority of shoppers are women but the majority of store managers are men. A new enlightened regime worked hard to change this, but after several months no change was happening. So the boss took a decision. He took one of the most promising female candidates and took away all of her targets for the first six months of her role as acting store manager. Without the immediate KPIs (key performance indicators) she flourished. When the measures were back in place, they found that she is now one of the most successful managers in the chain. Sometimes you have to break the rules to get talent to develop.

Wherever you go, you take the weather with you

Beware chasing a bigger role – if it sounds too good to be true, perhaps it is.

If you are unashamedly ambitious, that can be brilliant for your drive to get ahead, and, as we have seen, it may be less common in women than in men. This case study explains the importance of considering all the consequences of pursuing that ambition without thinking everything through.

Everyone wants a piece of Louisa: she's smart, fun to be around and she gets things done. Her contribution to her employers and her colleagues is enormous.

Louisa had worked at a company where she felt that her ambitions were being thwarted. She knew her value, but she was not progressing as fast as she wanted to. Her friends suggested to her that she had been held back due to the reputation of another colleague, someone whom no one had wanted to upset. When she asked her boss about promotion, he'd make vague sometime-in-the-future promises. He'd talk about the importance of not upsetting the balance in the company. He'd talk about how valued she was and say that it was just a matter of the right opportunity presenting itself. Louisa felt increasingly frustrated. She was doing her part to make sure that the company succeeded and achieved change. Yet she did not feel that others were. Despite the fact that her colleagues weren't doing the job that they were supposed to be doing to make change happen (perhaps the company had spread them too thinly across a number of tasks), everyone else was apparently happy with the status quo. When she tried to accelerate progress, her cards were marked. She was told that a woman colleague understood the pace of change better than Louisa, that she could deliver by consensus not by disruption, that she considered the needs of everyone in the team. Perhaps that she was more appropriately feminine. As far as Louisa was concerned, this meant that she allowed people off the hook and was part of the barrier to getting things done. Bored with being the understudy to a supposed star, whose style she did not emulate, Louisa decided to leave.

As if by magic, the opportunity arose that she had yearned for: a similar company needed her and had a gaping hole where her talents could flourish. She'd be part of a new team that was going to transform the place. She'd be in at the start, and she could shape her destiny. It was like being swept off her feet. She would be first among equals in the new company. She had a get-together with her new senior management team, and it was clear that all her future peer group were insistent that she join them. That they all believed that without her none of the transformation would be possible.

So she resigned, and went off to start the transformation. Big job, big title, big ambitions to achieve.

At first, all her expectations were met, and the momentum was with her. However, as time went on, little glitches started to appear. Aware of the scale of the transformation and not wanting to appear petty, Louisa ploughed on, hiring people to help deliver the change, doing just what she'd signed up for.

Increasingly, the team put in place to make the changes started to feel less like a gang of brave amigos and more like a random bunch with disparate intentions. A blame culture started to emerge. With results not matching expectations, everyone was questioning whether the direction they'd been taking was right. Louisa knew that transformations weren't instant and that to change direction would be a longer process – and she argued her case.

Finally, the chat that Louisa knew was coming took place.

Her boss took her aside and said that they'd maybe been too quick to change, that he was under pressure to put the brakes on, take stock.

The corporate ambition was too tricky for them, and the push-back was in place.

Faced with what felt like a cosmetic change of emphasis, Louisa thought about her own position and decided to leave. They'd hired her reputation, not the reality. They were too timid to achieve their goals. Looking back, she should have seen that. She had bought the dream. In her old role she had been convinced that the only barriers to her achieving her ambitions were her peer group. When she moved to work with a new team, she thought that everything would fall into place. Yet in reality and after reflection she realised that life is just not that simple. It isn't the ambition to change that delivers that change. It is culture; it is team trust; it is an understanding that change costs and that everyone has to pay. In this case it was just Louisa who had paid. She had chased the dream and not understood the consequences. She'd think hard about the culture in the next company she went to work for. She would look past the rhetoric and the title and think about the company's current trajectory.

We think that Louisa fell into the trap of mistaking aims for action, of confusing a set of great-sounding rhetoric for strategy and believing that she had the power to deliver change almost single-handedly. There is a lot of this kind of thing floating about in the world of business. This is the kind of higher-order-sounding claptrap that Richard Rumelt debunks in his book *Good Strategy, Bad Strategy*. Rumelt explains how bad strategy is often deployed as an excuse for real action. He cites four major hallmarks for bad strategy:

- fluff (impressive sounding gibberish and apparently esoteric concepts to create the illusion of high-level thinking);

- failure to face the challenge (if it is painful, we'll all just ignore it);

- mistaking goals for strategy (being the best place to work; increasing profit; being the go-to place for excellence – all great goals, none of them is strategy);

- bad strategic objectives (a long list of to-dos which again don't have meaning: for example, delivering transformational change, making all the work excellent, demonstrating the future of the sector).

He writes: 'Why is bad strategy so common? … It flourishes because it floats above analysis, logic, and choice, held aloft by the hot hope that one can avoid dealing with fundamentals and difficulties.'

Every single one of these hallmarks characterised the job that Louisa's ambition talked her into taking. If you take a role (as Louisa had done) with a list of supposed strategic goals and lots of enthusiasm, you may be colluding with a boss who wants the aim but not the pain. Don't be flattered into a role that fulfils your ambition immediately but which has no more substance than the fairy-tale ending of 'and they all lived happily ever after'.

AMBITION STRATEGY 6

Wherever you go, you take the weather with you

On the way up

As an individual, it's tempting to see the next big move (or any move) as the answer to issues with your current role. It's key that you make sure that your expectations are in line with where you plan to work. Obviously that changes over time but clarity is key – for both employer and employee.

From the top

Be careful what you wish for. If you're making ambitious hires, know that you have the scope to deliver on your promises.

Ambition in summary

In 2014 *The Huffington Post* painted a picture of the face of female ambition with a series of interviews of working women. They concluded that, of course, there was not one single aspect: female ambition has many faces. Yet time and again women spoke about pressures, about juggling, about work/life balance. There is an ambivalence in the face of naked ambition that, in contrast, more men seem to embrace. Women don't lack ambition. They are more complicated about it than men on the whole. In our series of case studies we have highlighted the importance of finding courage from within, of uncovering what motivates you, of unleashing your competitiveness, overcoming fear and using anger as an energy. There is also the story we closed with, of a woman whose ambition overrode her clarity of thought.

Ambition is not something to avoid; it's something that you must define for yourself. It is crucial to your career progression to be clear about what you will and will not do to move ahead. This does not need to resemble any blueprint, particularly not one of a predominantly male-led business. But it does need to be an authentic part of your personal brand – which we'll talk about more in the next chapter, on creativity.

Ambition: The strategies in brief

On the way up

1. Ask for what you want. Ask for the help you need.

2. Look at how the men around you behave. Don't let

yourself be left behind because they self-promote more aggressively than you do.

3. If you feel that your career path is blocked, if you feel that things aren't fair or aren't moving quickly enough, then break the rules.

4. If someone puts barriers in your way, use them as a leaping-off point. Use the energy that anger gives you to propel you towards your objective.

5. Feel the fear, then do it anyway. Don't let nerves put you off.

6. As an individual, it's tempting to see the next big move (or any move) as the answer to issues with your current role. It's key that you make sure that your expectations are in line with where you plan to work.

From the top

1. Beware the Peter Principle, and be aware that you might need to explain and encourage team behaviour.

2. Make sure that you encourage the women in your team to have a structured opportunity every month to tell you what they've achieved.

3. As a manager you have to be able to spot talent, even if it comes in an unconventional form.

4. If there is an unconscious gender bias in your business, then it needs to be uncovered. If fewer women are making progress than men, then frankly it probably means that this is the case.

5. Take the time to spot talent. If you can't see the talent in the quieter people – often that means the women – then slow down, try harder, look deeper.

6. If you're making ambitious hires, know that you have the scope to deliver on your promises.

Tessa is in her early thirties. She has had a rocket-like rise in her company, and is sure to be promoted further. She's decided to take a career break, as combining an ever more senior role with being mum to two toddlers isn't working for her. Her rise so far in her career has been very fast; all of her ambitions have been satisfied. Now she is genuinely conflicted between following the ambitious drive that she has had for her whole career and the needs of her young family. We speak to her as she is about to leave work for a sabbatical. She doesn't know yet when or if she's returning to her current role. She just wants space to think about it. We don't know what will happen and whether the choice that Tessa is making will prove a crucial turning point in her career, perhaps even an end to her chosen profession, or a reinvigorating and brief extended holiday or sabbatical.

'I guess where I am, I think, is that I have always been incredibly focused on progression in my career. First, reaching the board early at age twenty-six and getting to managing partner level in my early thirties. I think I'm just more confused about whether I want that sort of style of progression any more, and I'm not sure what I am motivated by. I have been really clear up to about two years ago that I want to be CEO or MD. I'm trying not to sound arrogant when I say this. I am aware that that's a big job, and it could take a long time to get there and I was very focused. Then after I had my second child I started to question that focus internally. What's become really clear to me more in the last six to nine months is I don't function very well if I don't know where I am going. I totally understand that I have created confusion for myself in terms of where I am going and I probably also hold in myself somewhere the answers to what I want to do and how I want my career to look or not to look, but I have never really dedicated time to thinking about it. I'm not sure how much self-awareness I have. This is really weird for me personally, as I have a really high emotional intelligence, but the one area that pulls it down slightly (but is still well above average) is self-awareness. So, really good empathy when it comes to other people, but not prioritising myself or putting clear time or boundaries around what I am willing to do and not do. Right now that is a massive challenge.

'When I was growing up, I had three really strong female influences in my life in totally different careers. Mum is the first one, and she was really successful in the fashion industry until I was about three or four, and she gave it up at that point. She always worked after that and was always focused on independence and doing well in what she did and ended up helping costume design and theatre plays at the local schools – she's a really strong stubborn and independent person. I also had my Auntie, who passed away twelve months ago. She had four boys really close, and she took about five years out of her career. I think the big thing about these two women is that my Auntie Mary was a mum in the late '60s and early '70s and she was the main breadwinner, and in that day and age that was a huge thing and it totally bucked society. And my Mum was obviously the same as that, so when Mum was doing her career in fashion, my Dad was a cab driver in London and ran a few cabs, but my Mum was the person that was in charge of the income that was coming in the house. I think those types of things in your background really influence you, and I am not sure that I ever questioned those roles. I just assumed that's what I would always do, and striving to be at the top within those roles was kind of what you did, and especially as a female. There was a real need to fight for my Mum and Auntie for them to do that at the time in society. My other influence came later and was my Dad's cousin Anthea, who is CEO of a shipping firm; she worked her way up from a PA, and she was a single mum. That culture is a very macho culture, and you have to be a certain type of personality to succeed. I came in contact with her when I was about eight, and now we are good friends. Those things shape you. It often means you follow a path they took without really analysing it, and I think having kids has probably made me think about it more. It makes you think about the choices you're making more than before. It was easier to ignore those questions in the past probably than it is now.

'My husband just wants me to be happy. That is quite hard – because it is hard when he says, "Be happy, do whatever you want to." "Be happy" is quite a difficult thing to hear or work through really. Then you have the guilt of self-indulgence. Well, you should be happy that you have a really good job with people you like spending time with and that your family are healthy and all of these things, so why that other side to yourself, where you are questioning all the time?

'Everything in my life got to crisis point in every bit of my life – little health things, that do affect you, to do with stress, and we moved out of London, which made it a lot harder to balance everything. I knew before we moved about that, and I did have quite a few doubts. I know this is the right lifetime decision for us and for the children in the long term, but for right here and now, given all the other pressures from our lives – family, health, husband's job security, x, y, z – it is just another thing to tip us over the edge.

'I pushed moving out of London because he would have walked away – and I said no, we are going to go make the decision. I said, "What are we waiting for? We should do it now", and I do realise that I have probably deliberately put myself in this position of having a long commute and more pressure.

'I'd wanted to move for a long time and then became really aware, with two boys, that I needed to move out of London, given what we could afford in terms of garden space. I could have waited easily and managed, and I probably should have talked about it earlier to the people that I work for. It is really hard to admit that you can't cope. It is really hard as a woman to admit that. I have in the back of my head a voice that says, "You do four days a week with loads of flexibility; you don't do all the stuff that your equivalent male colleague does; you don't go on trips to Manchester; and you don't do these extra things, so shut up and put up with the pressure." That voice sounds like one of those female role models (and sort of still my Mum a little bit). That voice says, "Are you sure? – These people, who you work with, love and care about you. Are you self-destructing? What are you doing?" But I think if my Dad was alive, he would have pushed me to have had this conversation earlier, as he was always a pragmatic voice of reason. He had that kind of good vision into people and emotional conditions.

'I actually really don't know what I am going to do now. I think I know that the only thing that I really do know, right now, is that I don't know whether I want to come back to work or not. It is fifty-fifty. I don't think that I will ever be long-term exclusively looking after the kids because I think I would probably become obsessive about the kitchen garden or create something ridiculous, you know, to self-combust over. But I think what is in my head is I need to stop doing three people's jobs and be really clear about what my boundaries are, what stimulates me intellectually, and make sure I have more time and space around positive influences in my life. I think I have struggled with that a lot, and I have never really thought about who I spend my time with or prioritise, and I think it is massively important.

'My husband has always been really good at that prioritisation, and I remember a conversation with him and his Dad when he wasn't well a year ago, and he spoke about certain people that he wasn't going to prioritise his time with. Although he loved them, it was difficult for him to see them; emotionally he felt drained after the interaction. And I have never thought about that until recently. And that's true of not just work and life, and I think it is important to put some boundaries in, or sort of do's and don'ts. So, I don't know is the answer.

'I lost the ability to take control at some point. It is a bit like the filter on what you hear from people who criticise you when you start taking it too personally. At a certain point I stopped saying: "No" and I started … I don't know what I started doing, but I just I can't do the stuff that I used to be able to do. I have to take a break and put my boys first.'

CHAPTER 2

CREATIVITY

*Men strut their stuff; women play
it down in order to conform*

Creativity: considered a feminine trait when it is concerned with macramé or baking; thought of as a masculine skill when concerned with hard-edged business innovation. Mary Berry or Martha Stewart versus Steve Jobs, perhaps?

Do you consider yourself a creative thinker, willing and able to find innovative solutions to the problems you encounter at work (and at home)? We personally know more men who would label themselves 'creative' in the sense of business innovation than women, but does that really mean that men are more creative problem-solvers than women? Or are men simply more comfortable with the unconventional, and better at claiming the 'thinking outside the box' space?

This matters, and does have an impact on how you are perceived at work, and whether your out-of-the-box thinking is seen as a benefit to the organisation or as random and erratic. In Duke University's 2015 research study participants associated creativity more with stereotypically masculine traits, including decisiveness, competitiveness, risk-taking, ambition and daring than with stereotypically feminine traits such as cooperation and understanding. When men took risks, they were called creative; when women took the same risks, they decidedly were not. The researchers concluded: 'This result suggests that gender bias in creativity judgements may affect tangible economic outcomes for men and women in the workplace.'

We can tell you that you are certainly a creative thinker if you are reading these words. It is a clear sign that you are looking for an alternative way to progress. That you understand that conforming to what is expected of you is not the only way to succeed (indeed, it may not be a way to succeed at all). If you are reading this chapter, then you are curious about how others have succeeded and want to pick up their techniques, and that is a sure indication of creative thinking in practice.

In the advertising industry there are departments called 'Creative', and notoriously they are largely run by men. These creative directors, or executive creative directors, are not necessarily the most creative or original problem-solvers. The creative work that they produce is often based on ideas that have emerged in other sectors, in film, in music, on vlogging sites on YouTube. Their skill lies in reaching the top of their profession by steering work to make it successful commercially. The most creative people we know often have very different titles: Chief Commercial Officer, Trading Director, Head of Insight, Chair, Chief Technology Officer. They may not call themselves creative, but when it comes to finding new ways of solving long-term problems, they are second to none.

One thing is definitely clear, however. If a man does decide that he is creative, then he will flaunt it. In some cases this flaunting expresses itself in rather obvious ways: he may dress differently from others in his company, donning jeans and brightly coloured T-shirts where others are in suits and ties. The Chief Creative Officer of one large engineering company never appears without a baseball cap where his peers are strictly formal in garb. Women, on the other hand, often feel less comfortable with the idea of unconventionality in the business environment. In some sectors their unspoken need to follow the rules means that they nearly always dress predominantly in black, never have bare arms or a neckline that dips below the base of the neck. Financial districts can be particularly noticeable for this.

Both genders suffer when they deny their latent creativity. It seems a particular shame when women do so, as they are often naturally highly creative. For instance, it takes a good deal of creativity to look like you are conforming in a male-dominated environment. It would be better to put in place ways of enhancing your creativity to come up with business-winning ideas than to use it to stifle your true self. There are guaranteed techniques that you can easily use which, with practice, will make you happily pronounce that you are a highly creative person and which will help with your prospects. For a business to be successful it needs a strong emphasis on creativity. The problems that it has solved in the past are not a template for the problems that it will need to solve in the future. Again and again senior management teams or boards are full of people who look and sound the same. This is no way to ensure that you are best armed as a business in coming up with new and unconventional strategies in competitive sectors. Instead, senior managers must encourage and incentivise their teams of people in creative development.

Here's one of the simplest, never-fail, techniques to adopt.

Borrow it

Tania had never been called creative in her life. Her mother is a painter and spent hours every day shut away in her studio. Tania, in comparison, clearly could not draw and always got bad marks in art class at school. Her elder sister had once told her that she was astonishing. 'In what sense?' Tania asked eagerly – at the age of eight any insight is appealing. 'Because you clearly have absolutely no imagination at all,' replied her sister. Even at eight this felt like a significant condemnation.

When she entered the workplace, it was after succeeding academically at analysis. Detailed, painstaking and thorough analysis was her modus operandi at work. She would ensure that at any meeting she attended she was the one who was best prepared. She worked hard at this, and would anxiously do her best to ensure that there were no surprises in store as much as she possibly could. Gradually, however, she came to see that this was not enough to get her noticed in the right way. So she began to think about what she was missing.

'I began to see that knowing more about the task in hand was not enough to get me noticed at work. Someone else would say something not that bright and not that well informed in the meeting, and the boss would praise him. I would be too nervous to speak up. If I speculated, how could that have value? I wanted everything I said to be informed by the facts. But other people were speculating and throwing ideas around wildly and getting praise for it.'

Tania, being Tania, started to approach the problem analytically. She read round the subject, and she paid close attention to the flow of behaviour in any meeting that she was in. She developed a strategy for two things that she could try. Both were quite intimidating. But, on the other hand, she was beginning to be very frustrated by her lack of career progress.

The first technique we've called 'Borrowed Brilliance' – a phrase used by one of our interviewees for this book: 'If we were considering a problem in our business, I would do some analysis of how someone in another sector had solved that problem, particularly if it was a brand that everyone admired. I started to give examples of what Nike, Google or Apple had done that I thought could be applied to our business issues. To begin with, people did not really get it, I have to admit, but I persisted and found that, if I made the example really simple and explained how it would work for us, then at least I was listened to.'

Rocket scientist and entrepreneur David Kord Murray believes that cherry-picking the ideas of others is vital for creative innovation. In his 2010 book *Borrowing Brilliance: The Six Steps to Business Innovation by Building on the Ideas of Others* he cites Isaac Newton's inquisition for stealing the idea of calculus, where Newton confessed: 'Yes, in order to see further I have stood on the shoulders of giants.' In other words, the plagiarist and the creative genius have pretty much the same techniques.

Tania's second technique was to speak up when she thought that instinctively she should be quiet. 'I had to force myself to do this. I would practise at home the night before. I would constantly say to myself: what is the worst that can happen? And although being snubbed in a meeting does feel awful and can be humiliating, because I was basing what I thought on good analytics – albeit from another sector – the worst never did happen. Instead, the very opposite began to occur. People began to look to me for an alternative point of view.'

Tania's way to solve the problem uses a simple technique

of creativity: applying a solution from one sector to another. Clearly this does not always work. Just because Google has built a successful business online does not mean that you should close all your bricks-and-mortar stores. Just because Nike runs advertising with football stars does not mean that you should forget that your brand appeals in an entirely different way to a shopper. But suggesting that the business makes its customer-facing products look beautiful in order to add desirability to function, as Apple has, is highly relevant.

Tania began to build a reputation for creativity to add to her rock-solid analytical credentials. She found that she was no longer only thought of as a safe pair of hands, as she had been in the past. Now she became the one who you could look to for new ideas. Yet Tania did not suddenly abandon her sense of wanting to know all the facts. She did not take to wearing a baseball cap and talking about the *zeitgeist* in an unintelligible way. Instead, she took her skill set and expanded it. She added to her personal brand.

This paid dividends for Tania. She had created a way for her voice to be heard. Her reputation grew as the one who was creative. Soon, in fact remarkably quickly, she became the one who the MD insisted came into the meeting, and, rather than have to fight for an opportunity to be heard, she was asked what she thought about the problem. All by simply applying her analytical brain to other comparable sectors. And much more creative than dressing in bright colours and wearing weird glasses or a hat.

Borrow it

On the way up

If you have an analytical brain and are good at the detail, this does not mean that you cannot be creative and build up your reputation in that area too. Keep looking at things logically and analytically. But expand your analysis from the niche arena that you specialise in to another related arena. Take the techniques that other companies have succeeded with, especially if they are companies that everyone admires, and roll them out in your meeting.

From the top

Every business needs to inject creativity into its problem-solving. There is still too much siloed thinking. Encourage everyone to believe in their creativity and to speak up with thought through opinion. Tania's MD was delighted when Tania plucked up the courage to look at issues through a different lens. Can you encourage your people in this and can you organise training in, and time for, 'Borrowed Brilliance' sessions?

CASE STUDY 2

Don't zig, zag

There are many interpretations of creativity. The traditional view of the genius artist permeates our perceptions. It also makes it a very hard measure to judge yourself by because, if it doesn't come naturally, then you're assumed not to have 'talent'.

Amy is a really diligent and detail-orientated person (just by reading that, you've just assumed that means she isn't creative, haven't you?). However, she loves working in ideas businesses, because she finds them stimulating. Her problem was that, despite her many excellent qualities, she was seen as someone who didn't contribute – her colleagues were mostly male, loud and excitable, and they wanted a kindred soul. We've written elsewhere about sport and the male/female divide; in this case, the phrase 'not part of the team' was used.

This created a dilemma for both Amy and her boss. He wanted her to be in the team, as she was the one who got things done and made sure deadlines were hit, but he also knew that she needed to be more active creatively or she'd be left behind. You know the score: people 'forget' to invite you to meetings, emails don't include you. If this were to happen it would freeze her out. The strategy they came up with has worked, and this is how they did it.

First, Amy read widely around her company's clients and their competitors. One of their clients was a wine importer, so she made sure she knew all the new restaurants that were planned, so that their distribution could expand and give the creative teams new projects to work on as they supported the launch. Over time Amy was the one who gave them the initial creative stimulus, talking about new sectors, trends and markets. The creative people peppered her with questions and asked for her to work as a filter for their output: she was the one who knew what would be right for the problem facing them and whether they could deliver it.

Then her boss changed where Amy sat in meetings about projects. She'd previously sat at the end of the table, pushing her chair slightly back, an observer. He placed her in the centre, where she quietly outlined the issue, the background to the briefing; and then he told her to write down all the ideas that were discussed, even ones that were dismissed by the larger group. The robust nature of the team meant that even good ideas were sometimes lost in the noise and more reflective analysis. Amy took a tip that a recruiter had given to her as a graduate, to be the one who, in group interview sessions, ensures that the ideas are carried through to action. It seems that young men never want to do that (they feel the observers will see them as too passive), whereas the company saw that volunteer as an enabler, able to park their ego. Just make sure that you're the one who is part of the presentation group at the end and that your role is acknowledged.

The learning from this is that you don't have to be the passive part of a creative process if you're not traditionally 'ideas and concepts' talent based. Quite often a team of creative people can come up with the totally wrong solution because they love their own idea so much that they don't stop to think whether it will work. Thinking about other ways of contributing can augment the process; your role needn't be to 'solve' the issue.

It is very easy to play to your inner doubts and decide that you aren't creative. The reality is that anyone who solves problems – be they ideas or people issues – is creative.

Don't zig, zag

On the way up

Amy had been pigeon-holed. Her persona is detail; her love is creativity. In the previous example we saw Tania find a way to add creative thinking through her analytical capabilities. In Amy's case she has added to the creative pool by being the one who makes things happen. Amy's capabilities here gave her a unique role in the team. Everyone else was running around brainstorming ideas. Amy did not join in with that chaos. Instead, she made the creativity real.

From the top

Every team needs rooting in reality. If all you have are creative self-styled geniuses floating around, then nothing really gets created. Amy's boss gave her status and credibility, and the whole team benefited.

CASE STUDY 3

Don't fear failure

Pragmatic. That's the word that we often use when we want to disguise our aversion to risk. It might be when you see a flawed but persuasively argued plan put into action, knowing you'll have to be part of the rescue pack sent in to retrieve it. You say to yourself, 'I didn't put my idea forward, I'm just being pragmatic. After all, they wouldn't have paid proper attention to what I suggested … I'll wait for the right moment.'

So you sit in another meeting, waiting for the moment when you can showcase your alternative idea. Two hours later it's still there, unspoken and in your head, as you walk back to your desk.

Women have a reputation for being generally risk-averse. We want to be accepted, part of the team, to have validation. We enjoy working with others, and if you were to be tempted to push the boundaries – well, who wants to make people uncomfortable? Not you. If you've got extensive experience, you're still unhappy at the prospect of saying, 'We did that before and it tanked' when someone suggests an innovative approach, even though the same approach did fail spectacularly in the past.

Alice works at a company where she only broke the cycle of 'pragmatic silence' because she was tired. Her baby daughter was on a run of waking in the night, and she was, in her own words, having 'an out of body experience'. Sitting in a room having yet another discussion about the seating plan at a dinner, she heard a voice say, 'Why don't we just get some people to move tables at the end of each course?' The voice went on: 'That way, more guests spend time with Tim and Carl (the heads of the company), and no one spends the entire night wondering why they're sitting where they are sitting.' Plus Tim and Carl don't get bored senseless with people sucking up to them or demanding a pay rise, she thought to herself. In normal circumstances Alice would never have said anything. (She saw her role as reassuring the people who weren't sitting near Tim and Carl that they were valued employees.) Alice also spent the night of the dinner on the table with people that no one in the management team wanted to sit with. It was, they explained, because she was so good with people.

As surprised as anyone that this voice was in fact hers, Alice sat back. She waited for the remarks that would blow the suggestion to pieces. Of course, they would be subtle – but surely it would happen.

A silence that felt like it lasted ten minutes fell over the room. Alice was too tired to provide more ammunition for her detractors, so she just sat there, oblivious.

Tim spoke: 'That's a great idea. Maybe this year I won't get indigestion as I sit through yet another pay rise request?' he laughed. 'Alice, if you could do all the diligence on the detail, we can all have a good time this year!'

Carl said, 'Alice, I love that idea. You, me and Tim should talk it through tomorrow.'

Luckily Alice got a proper night's sleep that night, and her follow-up meeting went well. She says now that she would never have done it if it hadn't been for her tired mind. She was always waiting for the chance to have the big, transformative idea that would make her stand out. Even as she had them, though, her inner voice would take them apart little by little until she thought they lacked consideration.

It can be really hard to be vocal about an idea. Our inner voice wants praise, recognition, group acceptance. Even when people say, 'In this room, there is no such thing as a bad idea', your inner cynic just laughs.

As Alice said, it was just a company dinner, and so her idea wasn't transformative. But it was a start, and now she feels that she can talk about her ideas because, the last time she did it, it was all OK.

Trust us, in most meetings people aren't thinking about anyone but themselves and their agenda. Male colleagues, when told time is tight and there's a lot to cover, will still go through their intended speech (and at length) even though it squeezes other colleagues' time slots. There's one colleague whom Alice now times against the clock (she has turned it into a jokey competition), owing to his love of recounting every detail of certain issues.

Failure is inevitable. You just have to embrace it. Learn from it and move on.

CREATIVITY STRATEGY 3

Don't fear failure

On the way up

Fear of failure makes you dry up, go dumb, be mediocre. Don't fear failure. What is the worst that can happen? We guarantee that it isn't that bad. Just go for it.

From the top

Never let any voice in the room be flattened by the noisy majority. Someone's burgeoning creativity should be encouraged. You never know when the person tentatively speaking up will become the next Peggy Olsen (the creative woman in TV show *Mad Men*) and step change the creativity in your business.

CASE STUDY 4

Tear it up

In his strikingly original 1998 book *The Alphabet versus the Goddess* the author and surgeon Leonard Shlain offers a theory to explain the patriarchy. He believes that it was the development of writing that rewired the human brain and developed a more analytical approach to solving problems. He argues that the 'feminine principle connects to images and the masculine one to written words'. As literacy became linked to power, as the alphabet developed, as religion was associated with the peoples of the book (the Bible), then the old goddess religions faded away and patriarchal religion took precedence. For millennia thereafter being a man meant that you had more power. So women developed roles instinctively to survive within that environment. However, get back to the real root of people's development around 2000 BC, and you find goddess religions where all of the power – birth, death, creation – comes from a female deity. Less logic and more instinct seem to be characteristics of certain styles of commonly acknowledged creativity. Shlain argues that this is more natural to a feminine archetype than a masculine one.

We know creative women who embody this creative power. We believe that it is buried deep within all of us – sometimes it needs a true revolution to bring it out.

Georgina is a great example to us all of this. She's not one for incremental changes. When she hits a problem, she tears everything up.

Georgina has had a number of firsts in her career. First woman head of a finance company. First woman in charge of a car business. First businesswoman in Russia after *Glasnost*. The list goes on. She believes that you have to be confident. She is a pioneer who is not afraid of disagreeing with the people around her. Nor is she afraid of trusting her instincts, even when she does not have empirical evidence to back them up.

This has meant that she has had a tough time selling her ideas to the people, mainly men, around her. 'I was booed at one company conference in the '90s when I foretold that the product we were selling would be sold on the internet.'

She does not mind being unpopular. If the business has hired her to take them from A to B, her approach will be to take them much, much further.

Georgina's thinking is that, if she has been brought in as a change agent, if the business has recognised that there is change coming, it usually means that everyone involved has finally, reluctantly, recognised this, and that almost inevitably it is nearly too late. Small changes will not at this point be enough. Course correction of a few degrees will not do. Georgina is inspired by turnarounds. She is the perfect person either for challenger brands or for established brands that are under threat from challengers. Her recipe for change is to ignore what is coming next and look at what is five years in the future. If she can deliver a revolution aimed at a time of real disruption, then she can drive a real creative advantage for the company.

Incremental change does not interest her. Seismic change is what is on the cards for any business that brings Georgina in.

She says: 'I always know what I want to achieve. People interest me, how they react. I can tell in minutes if I can get what I need from someone. I need people who will take that step with me and believe in me.

'I deliver change. This does not mean a perfectly detailed plan where every possible question is answered. Everything does not have to be perfect when you are writing a plan for wholesale change in the long term. It can't be. I will look at the big picture, and yes, build in safety nets for the possibility of things going wrong. There has to be an appetite for risk.'

Georgina's strategy is to surround herself with thinkers that are as ambitious and hungry for change as she is. Her start point is to work out the rules of the category that she is in. And then to see what would happen if she broke every single one of them. Out of this comes the beginning of the plan for change. Georgina tends not to stay with the business for longer than it takes to make sure that the change has happened, and that it has stuck. Maintaining the status quo does nothing for her, it doesn't interest her. She will create the revolution and then move on.

Advertising creative giant Dave Trott would argue too for the power of a total reboot when change is needed. He asserts that generally women have a tendency to overthink a situation: 'For women, it's every shade of grey. For men, if it's 49 per cent, it's white; if it's 51 per cent it's black.' He believes in binary thinking – that there should be a yes or no or an on or off decision at every point of the creative journey. He thinks that the fact that women care more about other team members' feelings is a distraction from getting a result.

We think it is a question of surrounding yourself with the right kind of support, as Georgina always makes a point of doing. Her radical and deeply *feminine* thinking applies not just to problem-solving but also to the process of delivering great work.

At one point, when she was working with a network of agencies and consultants, she refused to appoint the companies for whom her hand-picked team worked. She insisted on only working with named individuals and paying for their time, rather than contracting the firms that employed them. If those businesses did not agree, then they were out. And if they tried to substitute the named person, she wasn't interested.

Together her teams would look at every aspect of possible change, and take it as far as they could. They would break given rules of the category – imagine car advertising with not a car to be seen, or marketing for a product that was five years away from delivery.

Not everyone wants to work at this pace, but the strategy of establishing the rules that everyone in the category is playing by and then tearing up the main one is a great short cut to stand out and to differentiated thinking.

CREATIVITY STRATEGY 4

Tear it up

On the way up

If a creative solution is needed, then push the creative idea as far as it will go – push it to breaking point. Establish the obvious rules of the category, and then tear the most important one up. What ideas come out of this? You won't be able to deliver a perfectly justified plan for radical change, because if the idea is a truly original one, then it will lack empirical evidence. Dig deep – trust your instinct and ensure that you have enlisted supporters who will take a big step into the exciting unknown with you.

From the top

Don't stifle your original or creative thinkers. Give them room to experiment and, yes, to fail. Allow for their vision. Encourage big-picture thinking. In a business environment where rapid change and challenge are an everyday given, you need some room for ideas that might deliver a step change.

CASE STUDY 5

Be naïve

We are living proof that a little bit of naïvety in the face of conformity can give a creative spark.

In her early career Sue was working as a media planner on a pitch with a creative agency for Ajax Liquid cleaner. Her role was simply to decide in which magazines the advertising that the creative agency would write should appear. Although the budget for the campaign was a relatively small one, the client was prestigious, and winning the pitch was important.

Back in those days the pecking order between the creative agency and the media agency was clear and relatively unchallenged. Imagine the world of TV show *Mad Men* fast-forwarded to the last decade of the last century, and you wouldn't be far off. The media people had no status, and for a media woman – in general – that meant even less. But this creative agency had a different attitude from some. They wanted the whole team to contribute and to be behind the creative idea.

The product to be advertised had a unique selling proposition, which all the competing agencies were briefed about. It left no residue. So, unlike other products at the time, there was no need to wipe over the kitchen surface with a damp cloth after you had cleaned.

At the team meeting Sue showed a possible magazine schedule, and no one really commented. In those days, and with the money available, there was no other possible route to take, really, in order to reach the target buyers of the product: mainstream housewives.

The account director unveiled the creative idea. It showed a couple of housewives who had saved time by using Ajax Liquid and were learning to play golf. In another execution one was learning French. 'What do you all think?' asked the creatives who had come up with the advert.

Most of the room made encouraging noises. That's what you are meant to do in that situation. It's the thing that Sue probably should have done, given her status in the room – one of few junior women, the media person and one of the least senior by title.

But Sue couldn't stand to accept the status quo or the kind of behaviour that was due. She had a reason: she had just completed two weeks' research among housewives talking to them about how they felt about their portrayal in advertising. On the whole they felt negative. They felt that the way that they were portrayed meant they were either supposed to be incredibly glamorous or chained to the kitchen. They did not see cleaning kitchen surfaces as their job, whether they worked outside of the home as well or not. And the amount of time they would save from a quick wipe with a wet cloth (and only the minority of them would bother) would not afford them either the time or the money to learn a language or swan round a golf course.

She came out with her opinion – rather bluntly – partly through nerves and partly so that she could deliver it before the consensus in the room went with the current work. There was a pause, a dense silence. This wasn't meant to happen. The creative director had approved the ad concept. The junior media person was not supposed to disrupt the process only days before the pitch. Sue was not the expert in creating advertising. She had no experience in writing copy or winning pitches with creative advertising ideas. Her role was to justify whether six women's magazines should run the advertising or eight.

In that room, in that moment, she was the expert on how housewives felt about advertising. All she did was give her opinion on how they would react to the ad. Was it naïve? Yes. Was it the popular thing to do? No. The politic thing to do? No. Was it the right thing to do? Hell yes.

Now creative directors are intimidating at the best of times. They have their names on the doors of the agency. They don't suffer fools gladly. This creative director took a deep breath. 'Well, Sue,' he asked, 'if they don't want time to learn golf or French, what in your apparently expert opinion, is it that housewives want?'

Tough question. Sue off the top of her head simply gave the answer that she was sure the women she'd been talking to would give. 'What they really want is someone else to do the cleaning. And if you were to ask them in their dreams what they'd want, it would be someone else to do the cleaning, especially a gorgeous bloke.'

The meeting was over shortly after that. Next day – only the day before the pitch – Sue was called in. 'What do you think of this?' she was asked.

'I think it's brilliant.'

This was the Ajax Houseproud Hunk advert. It showed a gorgeous bloke cleaning the kitchen with the headline 'Save time cleaning, get him new Ajax Liquid'.

The agency won the pitch, the advertising ran and did well, sold lots of product and also led to a spate of men shown doing the cleaning in other adverts too. Also, because of its relative success, lots of people claim to have created the idea. The story described here is just Sue's version.

All Sue did was voice the naïve opinion of the target audience. She had found herself in the situation where she could best represent them. Speaking up for women in general can often fall to the women in the room, whether it's in advertising, retail, travel, finance or entertainment. In most households it is a woman who is making purchase decisions. Yet most boards of most companies are dominated by men. One way of getting noticed for your creative contribution at work is simply to be the voice of the typical purchase decision-maker in the real world.

CREATIVITY STRATEGY 5

Be naïve

On the way up

Say what you think. Be the voice of women in general in the real world. Do speak up, and don't conform. Too many companies make decisions on the basis of what has worked in the past and what suits them to manufacture or sell. Great advantage can be achieved by a switch inspired by the fresh approach or a different point of view.

Take the time to walk a few miles in the shoes of the target market. Imagine their experience and then feed that into the decision. As a woman, it is one way to play to your strengths, especially if you are in a minority in your team. While it might also play to mistaken stereotypes, if it gives you an edge then don't be afraid to use it.

From the top

Encourage non-conformity in your team members. Encourage them to step outside of the workplace and experience the sector as a consumer in the real world. If you hear a tentative view that challenges the status quo, then listen and act on it.

Creativity in summary

In Chinese philosophy yin and yang are opposite forces that interact to form a dynamic system in which the whole is greater than the assembled parts – where creativity is born. Traditionally gender is assigned to these forces. Yin is dark and feminine, and yang is light and masculine. You need both aspects to create, and they must be complementary rather than in opposition. There is no hierarchy. Masculine energy is not better than feminine energy in this respect. Nor do you have to be a man to access yang or a woman to access yin. Everyone has a mix of yin and yang qualities in different amounts. It is never our intention in this book to assert that women and men are the same: clearly they are not, as our research and interviews have shown. Yet traditional judgements about masculine qualities being 'better' in some respects, whether for creativity or in other ways, seem to linger. Culturally people still make judgements, as the research in the introduction to this chapter shows. Is masculine creativity different from feminine creativity then? If it is, it is no more or less valuable to business, and we believe that every creative person needs to play with both types of energy in order to innovate. Play is important. You may have to lighten up sometimes. Albert Einstein said: 'Play is the highest form of research.' You do not always have to be serious in order to be taken seriously. You need to have a reputation for more than pragmatism and analysis in order to get ahead. There are many ways of exercising creativity, and it annoys us considerably when it is regarded as the preserve of an elite (masculine or otherwise). Embrace your own way of being creative, and you will find that it is a useful stepping-stone to the career you deserve.

Creativity: The strategies in brief

On the way up

1. Borrowed brilliance from another category or field is a great, relatively simple way of injecting creative thinking.

2. If everyone is heading in one direction and has a single consensus – go the other way. When they all zig, you should zag.

3. There are many things to fear in life. Failure in a meeting is not one of them. Expect to fail sometimes, intend to fail sometimes. If you don't, you're never going to learn anything.

4. Push the idea till it breaks.

5. Be naïve, ask the stupid questions, listen to your gut instinct.

From the top

1. Encourage everyone in the team to think of themselves as creative. Don't let it be owned by an elite team – bring out the creativity in everyone.

2. If there is a consensus that is sweeping everyone in an unchallenged direction, encourage the lone voice that puts forward another point of view and hear what they have to say before signing off for the majority decision.

3. Encourage the team to believe that they have permission to screw things up sometimes. An environment where

no one ever fails means an environment that stifles any creative leaps.

4. Support those in your team who tend towards big-picture thinking – incremental evolution needs to be balanced by big paradigm shifts sometimes.

5. Allow the naïve questions – just because conventional thinking is established, that doesn't mean that there isn't a different route.

ONE VOICE: KELLY

Kelly is a single mother and has a full-time job. At the moment she lives near her parents, who help significantly with childcare, but it is a long, long commute to the office. Her current circumstances have proved impossible, so she has tried to be creative about the situation. She is taking a bit of an out-of-the-box solution to the problem and cutting the ties with her home. She's about to move nearer work, but with the benefit of the shorter journey comes a new problem of being isolated from her personal support network.

'So I work full-time, I am a single parent and it is tough. Really, really tough. I have been trying for the last two years, to try to move to London to be nearer my work. But it comes down to finances and support for my child, because my family are in Suffolk. I have tried to speak to work, obviously, about all sorts of different working arrangements. The business I work for doesn't like four-day weeks. So I am full-time, although I actually quite like it. I enjoy working full-time. I like the fact that I am going to lead my daughter into that way of thinking, that you work hard for what you get. Nothing is given to you. I like that. I have always been that kind of character.

'I don't get any maintenance from her father. I have a mortgage, and I am trying desperately as a working woman to be recognised in my job, to do really, really well. I want to do well, and I have that desire. But at the same time I am a mother. I do want to go home and put her to bed. So there is that juggle. I am aware of looks over people's computers: 'Why she's going early?' Or 'Why is she leaving at five?' I have a two-and-a-half-hour journey home. So I leave on time to put my daughter to bed, because if I don't my parents do, and then they become more parents than I am. I am trying, as I said, to manage everything, to give her a good home, to give her a good start in life – to give her the best possible start in life because I know how difficult it is. I want her to really feel that she can look up to me and know that

I have been that pillar of strength. I haven't just given up (and it is easier to give up).

'I could walk away from my job and probably be better off. If I surrendered my mortgage and went and got benefits as a single parent, I would spend more time with my daughter, and, OK, we wouldn't have the luxury goods, we wouldn't go on holiday, but I would actually be better off, due to my commuting costs and everything. When I come to work, I try to focus and try not to think too much about home, because I want to be recognised in my profession as doing a good job. And I think I have struggled with that to start with, in my job, because people didn't know I was a single parent, so I got very judged on why I was leaving at five o'clock in the afternoon, I wasn't staying to the end of the day every day and I wasn't out every night with work … it wasn't until people got to know me and they found out that I was a single parent that it became a lot easier. Life isn't easy, at all.

'I am just about to embark on a move to London, finally. Six weeks' time.

'Which is going to be horrendous. It's going to be horrendous because my daughter goes to school this year, so she finishes school at half-past three. I have then got to factor in that she is going to have to go to after-school club, and I can't go and pick her up because it is just not acceptable. I will be an hour and a half away from my family. It has been a massive decision.

'I am moving, and it should help me spend more quality time with my daughter. I should be home at half-past five to cook with her and do the things I should be doing as well as doing a full-time job. But it doesn't mean to say I don't respect my job just because I am a mother. I do. My business has gone through a restructure recently, with opportunities for promotion. I felt that I had to take my boss to one side to say that the reason why I wasn't applying for the next level was that I am a single parent and I can't give the extra hours, at the moment, that I feel a management role needs. I did feel under pressure to make that known, so that they didn't just think that I didn't care about the job, because I do.

'I am not the only mother. I am the only single parent. When I ask for more flexibility, they say that, if they do it for one, they have to do it for everybody. I have never challenged it because I respect the people I work for. I wouldn't want to be seen as a trouble-maker, either. I am grateful for my job, so, again, I don't want to rock the boat. We are in a sales role, we are customer-facing. I know what I am like. I work on my holiday, I can't help it. I don't mind working from home, or at the weekends.

'I don't want to fail in my job because I am too tired, because when I get home I have got to read my daughter a story and make my own dinner, and by the time I am get to bed it is ten o'clock and I haven't had any time to myself to unwind or think about my day or to think about work. So it's, it's hard. It really, really, is. I am not saying it as an excuse; it's just difficult to manage. I am doing my absolute best not to ask anyone for help.

'I don't tell my managers it's a struggle. Partly because they are men, and therefore I am not sure they would totally understand anyway. Because they come to work, and their wives deal with every-thing. So I have never sat down and said: "Guys this is bloody hard. I want to work, I want to do well, I need you to help me here, I need to learn this side of the business, but I haven't got time to learn this side of the business. I am over here trying to juggle being a mum, and equally I can't just chuck my daughter to a child-minder and expect her to see someone else more than me." No, in that respect I have not sat down and spoken to them. I wouldn't know where to start with them.

'I think, coming back in to my job after I had had a baby, I knew the industry I would be in would be very corporate. I have a friend who works in a company that is run by women; it is refreshing. Especially around Christmas, when the business allows mums to come in with their children. The reception is a hustle and bustle of buggies, parties, senior members of staff getting involved, and you are not feeling like you are in the way. Whereas, the industry I am in, our Christmas party is not cut out for children.

'In an ideal world I would love to have a flexible working week. I would love to be able to say that it's OK to go and work from home in the afternoon, if all you are doing is admin. My main client was closed for the period between Christmas and New Year last year. I travelled two and a half hours to sit at my desk, pretty much, and tidy up. Where I could have been at home with my daughter. Even working from home and taking calls. That could be something that would be amazing.

'I would hope it will change. I hope it will change and people don't think of you any differently as a working single mum. I am a mum, it doesn't make me any less intelligent. It doesn't make me worthless just because I'm a mum. I have still got stuff to add. Even if I were extremely wealthy, I wouldn't want to be a stay-at-home mum. I have my own goals and I really, really, want to do well in my career. No matter what that is, I want to be successful, at whatever level that is, and be able to look my daughter in the eye and tell her that is how it's done, don't give up, you keep going. Because it is easier to give up.'

CHAPTER 3

CUTTING THROUGH

*Men like to be noticed; women
like to get on with the work*

Time and again our interviewees for this book have talked to us about a striking and significant difference between men and women when it comes to being noticed.

It's probably true that the best thing to be noticed for when you start out is an adequate level of competence, of not screwing up. If anyone in their first year spends too much time worrying about coming to the attention of the senior management, it can really jar with the more experienced staff, who would just like them to get on with what they're asked to do. We remember giving some mentoring to a young man in his first year of his career. We rattled through a list of five or six things that we wished we'd known when we'd started out. He didn't really seem to be paying much attention. So we asked him if he had any questions. 'Yes,' he replied, 'what's the best way to get into a meeting with the CEO?' Wrong question. How to get noticed by the CEO for contributing to the business success of the company – that's a better one. A desire to fast-track your career progression is not a bad thing, but a start point has to be delivering what you're being asked for. In our book, that's based on learning your job and over-delivering before you try to get noticed.

That said, we do see around us, time and again, women who think that doing the job well is all you need. This is equally wrong. It is well documented that, while women start out on equal footing with men in most workplaces, their career trajectory lacks speed after their late twenties. Many people automatically put this down to maternity leave. Statistics do not back this up. Instead, it's much more likely to be a confidence issue.

US authors and broadcasters Katty Kay and Claire Shipman write:

> Some observers say children change our priorities, and there is some truth in this claim. Maternal instincts do contribute to a complicated emotional tug between home and work lives, a tug that, at least for now, isn't as fierce for most men. Other commentators point to cultural and institutional barriers to female success. There's truth in that, too. But these explanations for a continued failure to break the glass ceiling are missing something more basic: women's acute lack of confidence.

This is bad news. The good news is that confidence is something that you can learn. In fact, if you fake it, you can make it. Here's how.

What trainers do you wear when you exercise? The ones with the swoosh?

What car do you drive? What does it say about you?

What's your favourite drink?

We are surrounded by brands, and we identify ourselves by them, whether consciously or not. From what we wear to what we eat and drink, everything says something about you. Big companies have been exploiting this for years to make a profit. It is absolutely possible that the trainers you choose have a specific advantage over a cheaper brand. But you probably wouldn't notice. If your drink of choice is lager, then you're definitely in the market of buying the label. And as for bottled water, try a blind taste test with iced tap water. See if you can really tell the difference.

People like brands. They even love them. Utility and practicality are one thing. The label is another and, in some sectors, way more powerful.

There's plenty of power in this for big corporations. There is also plenty of potential power in this for you if you can define and market your own personal brand.

Business author Tom Peters, writing in *Fast Company* magazine, tells everyone to ask a series of questions about themselves:

> What is it about yourself that you are most proud of?
> What is the 'feature-benefit model' that the brand called
> You offers? Do you deliver your work on time, every
> time? Your internal or external customer gets dependable,
> reliable service that meets its strategic needs. Do you
> anticipate and solve problems before they become crises?
> Your client saves money and headaches just by having
> you on the team. Do you always complete your projects
> within the allotted budget?

Ask yourself what it is that you want to be famous for.

CASE STUDY 1

Brand yourself

Sabrine went through this process at a key moment in her career. She is one of the senior leadership team at a global consultancy firm. Fewer than 10 per cent of the people in her role are female; in fact, the current figure is the all-time high for her company. She is often the only woman in the meeting. Getting her promotion was tough. Not just difficult, but emotionally tough too. She was put on a coaching programme in her late twenties that was unlike anything that she'd experienced at work before. The purpose of the course was to discover her personal brand.

Up until that point Sabrine had been a hard worker, very diligent and very effective. She didn't waste time on softer skills at work: in a more traditional environment this is rarely encouraged in women. As many women do, she had reached a fairly senior middle-management level by getting results and being highly competent. It now felt as though the next promotion was taking too long, and so Sabrine jumped at the chance of the coaching when it was offered to her.

'I received 360 degree feedback. Not just from my co-workers. From my best friend, from my parents and from my husband. This made me realise that I was a completely different person at work. It was a really important intervention for me. There was such a dichotomy between my home self and my work self. It was really quite traumatic.'

Sabrine had played to the stereotypes at work until this point. She had been an *über*-tough female in a predominantly masculine environment, and she had done this at the expense of her authenticity. When forced to examine how she presented herself at work, and put through the process of deciding her personal brand, she opted for authenticity above all else.

She changed how she dressed, how she behaved in meetings, how she interacted with her team and her colleagues. She began meetings by being friendly. She found out about her team's personal lives and ensured that she enquired about weekends, children, parents and holiday plans.

Out went dark and masculine suits. Sabrine brought **all** of herself to work now.

This was quite a change for her, and her management style.

She became honest about having to take time to work from home if her baby was poorly. When she needed help, or didn't understand something, she would ask a question, when in the past she might just have been keen to move the subject on. Overall her new brand, Brand All-of-Sabrine, is a much more successful one, and she finds that people go out of their way now to cooperate with her. Sabrine won success by bringing her charming home self into the workplace to counterbalance her edgier, more acerbic, work persona.

'I perform better when I am myself. I see women holding themselves in check all around me. Women have self-limiting conversations with themselves all the time. They are less happy to wing it. They seem less driven by ambition and more by what they are sure they can do. If they aren't able to ape the men around them in a masculine-driven environment, they talk themselves out of the next promotion.'

Authenticity as a brand attribute is easy to say and sometimes hard to deliver. Time and again the women we've spoken to have said how essential it is – for success at work, but also for a happier time overall.

Remember, however, that although bringing all of you to work is important, and a good place to start, it is not the only brand attribute in Brand You that you can go for. You could set out to be famous for being a 'safe pair of hands'. You could choose the subject of the last chapter: 'creativity'. Maybe being ultra-feminine or ultra-macho will suit you. The idea is to commit to a brand persona. Identify with it, work out what it means that you would or could say, dress or do differently. Then go out of your way to become famous for it.

Brand yourself

On the way up

Have a look at Tom Peters's work on your personal brand. How would your colleagues describe you? Is that a formula for success? Would you promote that woman? What would your nearest and dearest outside work say about you? Is that more authentically you? In your job, in your sector, what is the most valuable role you could play that also plays to your strengths? Stop seeing your career as something entirely personal. Take a step outside yourself and see what the best brand you can build for yourself might be. Then make sure that everything you do or say (or wear) at work aligns with it.

From the top

Talented hard-working women in your team will not necessarily have any idea how to get themselves noticed. Formal training is one idea to help them, although the right mentor, outside the company, could also be the person to help them look outside themselves and consider their personal brand.

CASE STUDY 2

Speak their language

Sara strode confidently into Jim's office. She had a brilliant idea for him. They'd worked together for months now and, although he'd recently been promoted to managing director, and therefore was now her boss, she was more than sure of herself and that he respected her opinions.

'You know the problem we've been having between the different teams here, Jim?

'Well, I've been thinking about it, and I'm sure I have a solution. Let me organise a Role Reversal course, where for two days everyone swaps jobs. I think that could make a real difference in understanding between departments and seriously improve the relationship between teams.'

Jim looked at her. He seemed angry.

'No, Sara, that's a terrible idea. The whole problem here is that there's a real lack of focus. If you start explaining to people other people's jobs that is just going to make the situation much worse.'

Sara edged out from Jim's office. Pretty miserably.

That afternoon Sara started to dwell on what had just happened. She could see different ways of reacting laid out in front of her. She felt as if she was at a crossroads.

She was tempted to react angrily. She could throw her hands up in the air, acknowledge that her new boss wouldn't or couldn't listen to or respect her ideas and get straight on to a recruiter to find her a new job. She could pick the phone up right now; only recently she had turned down an approach about a new role because she was excited about working for Jim. Not now. She felt unappreciated. She felt unloved.

She could try harder with her idea. What if she spent the evening researching the topic and putting some proper analysis behind it? Perhaps her big mistake was to have bounced it off Jim so casually. Maybe he needed proper data? By working late that night she could put together a presentation that would add substance to her ideas, including a selection of slides of comparable case studies that had all demonstrated a good outcome and return on investment.

Or she could buy a friend a cup of coffee and have a moan.

This is what she did. When she explained her idea in a sentence or two, and how Jim had reacted, her friend made a suggestion: 'Did you tell him that it's like Dutch Total Football from the 1970s?'

'What's that?' Sara replied.

Her friend explained that in the 1970s the Dutch national football team trained every player to play in everyone else's position. They were very successful. Most men who have any interest in football, whatever their age, know exactly what Total Football is and how successful a tactic it can be.

So Sara knocked on Jim's door the next morning.

'You haven't come back again about that stupid idea have you, Sara?' he barked. (He was never at his best first thing.)

'It just occurred to me that it's a bit like Dutch Total Football from the 1970s,' Sara replied.

'That's brilliant,' said Jim unexpectedly. 'That will give us a real competitive advantage. How soon can you organise it?'

Sara used a tactic here that many women in her position might have overlooked. Rather than be knocked down by the setback, or allow her confidence to be undermined, she instead came up with the correct language (in this case, a football analogy) to get her point across. She didn't fall into the trap of working all night and finding data and analytics to present. This still wouldn't have persuaded her boss. In fact, she hadn't done any more work at all. She had simply presented her idea to Jim (thanks to her friend) in a language that meant he could instantly appreciate its value.

Jim himself would have been mortified if he had under-stood what had happened, and what he had inadvertently done. He had made a valued colleague feel unwanted by his brusqueness – brusqueness that was in any case as natural to him as breathing, but if anything was more prevalent given his affection for Sara. He thinks of her as a friend, not just a colleague, and for that reason didn't think that he had to hide his feelings from her. He didn't understand that his promotion meant that he needed to be more careful with how he treated her now that he was managing director.

If she had walked out on him, he would have lost one of his most trusted and useful team members. Anyone in his position needs to be sensitive how someone that works for them might react to the situation and properly account for it. Jim was lucky – and one day Sara should explain why.

CUTTING THROUGH STRATEGY 2

Speak their language

On the way up

It is easy to mistake a rejection of your suggestion as a rejection of the idea. Of course it is. More often than not the rejection is a rejection of the format of the idea, not of the content of that idea. The format of any suggestion is as important as the idea itself. In this instance Sara bounced back from an outright rejection by using a football analogy. It is so simple, but it was just luck that she arrived at it. Before you take an idea to your boss, think about the very simplest way that you can explain it. Find out what they're passionate about – it might be sport, it might be art, it might be education. Use the language of their passion to explain your thinking.

From the top

Managers are by nature busy. Left-field suggestions can feel like an intrusion into a busy, efficient workplace. On the other hand, they might be the most brilliant way for you to get an advantage over your competition. Organising a time to be open to ideas from other sectors, or counter-intuitive thinking, might be the best way to drive your business. Whether this is possible or not – be clear about the fact that, if you do turn someone down who's trying to suggest a change, you need to be as encouraging as possible or they won't come back with another idea, ever.

Ha ha: be funny

Creative director Dave Trott has a joke about gender difference at work. He says 'Men insult each other all the time at work; but they don't mean it. Women compliment each other all the time; but they don't mean it either.'

There seems to be a very different set of rules for men and for women around humour and around so-called banter. Do women take 'funny' seriously enough as a career-boosting technique? Do men allow them to?

Being very good, very eloquent, very efficient – these are all great qualities for your career. Good use of humour can give you a boost like nothing else, however, and help you stand out from the crowd.

Andrea had prepared, prepared and prepared for her big conference. There was one gaping hole in her preparation, though. She didn't have any jokes.

Andrea has been asked to speak at a conference debate for her industry body. The topic, a hot one for the business world in general, was 'Who will make the most of big data?'

Andrea is in her late twenties and a data manager for a medium-size corporation. She feels she is on the brink of a career breakthrough. This is still an unusual job for a woman, and she's proud of her company and the work it does. This is a great opportunity to represent them, and she has ensured that all of her senior management will be present. She knows that they have some doubts about her gravitas and authority, and this is a huge opportunity to win the debate (the audience votes after hearing the three speakers) and to show her leadership and inspirational abilities to her bosses.

The talk is scheduled for Monday night. Everything is in place. Andrea has produced slides that talk about her company's use of data; there is a rigorous argument about its advantages and proof point after proof point. She has rehearsed her speech. She knows her stuff. Surely there is only one outcome to the debate. A win for Andrea, lots of glory for the firm, a definite promotion at the turn of year.

This is not exactly how the evening went.

There were three speakers. Andrea was sandwiched between two men. Up comes speaker number one. He's a Glaswegian. (We mention this so that you can imagine the accent as he delivered his speech.) This is how he begins his talk:

'Good evening everyone. I am very pleased to be here tonight. I frequently get asked about data because I used to work in America for a company that specialised in finding insights in data. The company was called American Research Systems. The product – the report – was also called American Research Systems, or ARS for short. Now you may or may not know, ladies and gentlemen, but the Americans do not ever use the expression "arse". They speak of the "ass", not the "arse". Therefore when my colleagues were talking about the key product that American Research Systems had developed, they would often refer to it by its initials very happily, but as one word. Most days then someone would say to me, "Have you see the latest ARS for the client?" I would happily reply, knowing that only I got the joke: "No, I haven't seen the latest ARS, but as soon as I do I will get properly and fully stuck into it!"'

By this point the audience – there to judge the presentations – were laughing uproariously. One man in the front row could hardly keep his seat for laughing. It didn't matter after that what the rest of the first speaker's presentation consisted of. (He had great points to make, of course, but that was hardly the issue.) He'd already won the debate. Andrea's speech was fine, logical, earnest and eloquent. Had no jokes, no jokes at all.

She learned a lesson here. If you want to win over a conference audience, or indeed any audience, humour can be a great tool – particularly, we believe, from a woman. For two reasons. First because, in our experience, humour is less frequently used by women. Not many women will put as much effort into preparing the joke as they will into preparing the slide deck. In this instance our first speaker certainly had. For a mixed-gender audience there is a second reason: in our interviews for this book it became clear that many men do not think women are funny. Not at work anyway. It is part of our 'mystique' to them. Men take funny seriously. They communicate via the use of humour. In this not uncommon, but often unspoken, masculine view of the world women don't. Men insist that humour is crucial to how they bond with each other. They say women are not funny.

The philosopher Simone de Beauvoir wrote over six decades ago about the desire men have to maintain a difference between genders:

> Of all the myths none is more firmly anchored in
> masculine hearts than that of the feminine 'mystery'.
> It has numerous advantages. And first of all it permits
> an easy explanation of all that appears inexplicable.
> The man who 'does not understand a woman' is happy
> to substitute an objective resistance for a subjective
> deficiency of mind; instead of admitting his ignorance he
> perceives the existence of a 'mystery' outside himself: an
> alibi, indeed, that flatters laziness and vanity at once.

We all have an element of mystery. A lack of openness. Everyone is entitled to present their best self in the workplace and, although being authentic is important, you don't have to bring the kitchen sink to work, whatever your gender. Humour in the workplace is one way of cutting through the competition and getting a profile that will bring you a more senior role. No one, male or female, should be telling you to suppress your sense of humour.

For men humour can be competitive. They call it banter. This is understood between men at work at a very basic level. When a man enters a meeting, he will instinctively summon up a bit of banter for each of the other men in the room – a humorous put-down of some kind. He might not say this out loud, but he may be thinking of his companions: 'Shorty, Scouse, Speccy, Softy', etc., etc. (the nicknames and insults obviously do not have to be alliterative). Women usually do not do this. This is not how they think of the people around them in a meeting. This is not usually how they bond. They do not expect to be insulted, even by banter, in any way by the others in the meeting. This does not mean, however, that they do not have a sense of humour. If you encounter this level of banter and find it off-putting, just have a quiet word. It will have leaked out, often by mistake, and you do not have to put up with it.

For women humour can give them the edge. It cuts through because it is still unexpected. It is a leveller. Put as much effort into your use of humour in a speech, or any meeting, as you do into the rest of the content.

Ha ha: be funny

On the way up

Think of use of humour as a way to get noticed, but make sure that you're being noticed in the right way. If you need to put someone down who is attacking you, then frankly an appropriate dose of banter can be very powerful. When you open up a debate, or begin a speech, try a joke to settle the room and get people on your side. It does not matter whether they laugh out loud or not (never, ever wait for a laugh). But put the same thought into your opening joke as you do into the content of your presentation.

From the top

Advice for male senior managers specifically is that you need to understand at a conscious level that your more junior female colleagues do not have the same understanding of banter or humour at work as you do necessarily. This does not make them mysterious. Nor does it make them unfunny.

Diversity in humour in the workplace is important. For any manager, male or female, the jokes you dispense to bond the team had better work for all concerned, or you will just end up with people who are exactly the same as you. Your job is to make sure that everyone feels a part of the organisation. Encourage use of inclusive and appropriate humour among your team.

CASE STUDY 4

Shhhh: cutting through as an introvert

Confidence and assertiveness at work are an essential part of cutting through. However, they are often confused with being an extrovert. Many popular quizzes that test confidence levels will ask the kinds of question that actually distinguish between introverts and extroverts. If you are the former, you will feel like you have failed the test. In fact, quiet confidence in your own competence and the ability to assess your expertise are not wrapped up in extroversion. If you are more introverted, and this case study is especially relevant to you, then you need to find your own way of cutting through quietly.

In her excellent book *Quiet: The Power of Introverts in a World that Can't Stop Talking* Susan Cain describes the setback of natural introversion at work like this: 'Introversion … is now a second-class personality trait, somewhere between a disappointment and a pathology. Introverts living under the Extrovert Ideal are like women in a man's world, discounted because of a trait that goes to the core of who they are.' As if being a woman wasn't enough of a barrier in an environment dominated by men, then, now let us add, for many, the pain of introversion.

Introversion and extroversion: the difference between whether you are inner- or outer-directed; whether you get most reward perhaps from knowing in your heart that you have done the best job you can, or only if your good work is recognised by others, from their praise and attention. How do you know which you are? Myers Briggs is one well-known professional profile system that will diagnose you, if you can take their test. Alternatively you can ask yourself how you respond when you're sober and someone suggests karaoke. If you run for the ladies' toilet, then you're definitely an introvert. If you prefer one-to-one encounters when you socialise to holding court in a crowd, then the same is probably true. Susan Cain believes that introverts (among which one of your authors is definitely included) are wired differently. The very stimuli that cause anxiety to the introverts reward the extroverts with a dopamine high. She also believes that in the public arena and in the world of most employers the extroverts are winning. If too much public attention does make you shrink inside, then how do you cut through in the workplace?

If you are an extrovert, by the way, you can probably skip

this case study – just be grateful that, whatever other challenges you're facing in your career, this is not one of them. On the other hand, given that we are all on a continuum of degrees of introversion/extroversion (again, just like masculinity/femininity), then you might want to read on.

We pick up Marianne's story when she is approaching a senior management position in a small but flourishing business. She has reached the point that she is at because of her diligent and detailed work. Now she feels that her career has stalled. The whole board is male: is that why? In addition, the whole board are extroverts. At the office Christmas party games that involve the senior managers dropping their trousers are not uncommon. Drinking games led by the directors are mandatory. When Marianne thinks of hosting the party under these conditions, she is not even sure that she wants the next promotion. Yet she is ambitious. She likes the company. She knows that she is doing well. She needs to find a way to make the next promotion inevitable.

She does not believe that she will ever solve the problem by becoming more like one of the boys. It is just never going to happen. She can't fake it. Indeed, she found the last office party verging on the traumatic in terms of public displays of bad behaviour and found every excuse to skip the next one, something that did not go unnoticed by the MD and chairman and which cost her points in their estimates of her possible leadership qualities.

She uses a regular catch-up with a respected friend who is in a senior management role at another company to air the problem discreetly. 'I'll never make it to the board at this rate. The boisterous behaviour of the board is not something that I can fake. Whether it is the banter, the boasting or the rows – none of it is me.'

Her friend Hilary gives this some thought. 'My advice to

you is to introduce the whole senior management to personality coaching. If the business has never tried that approach, then it may well unlock more potential for the company than just your very well-deserved promotion. You know that there are government grants for medium-to-small businesses for investment in people, so the cost of this need not be a barrier.'

This turned out to be brilliant advice on a number of levels. It gave the very able men in the business a way to understand diversity better. It gave Marianne a role in improving the business overall rather than just excelling at her known and specific objectives. If you are seeking promotion at a senior level, it is essential to do something over and above your key ascribed tasks. Understanding herself and her colleagues better also gave Marianne an enormous boost in confidence. She recognised that the fact that she did not want to join in with every bit of organised fun was not a failing, and that there were others in the firm who would prefer not to as well. This in turn boosted her overall confidence, which meant that she asserted herself more in terms of her core competencies. And that she began to walk tall when in the past she might have tried to keep a low profile.

Susan Cain suggests that, once you have recognised that you are an introvert, you should enter into a pact with yourself: a 'free trait agreement'. If your role or next promotion requires a certain amount of networking, then agree the terms with yourself. You do not have to go out every night. (That's what the extroverts are for!) But perhaps agree (with yourself) to commit to a networking evening once a fortnight. At that evening you will enter into at least one deep conversation with someone new (because that is easier for you) and then follow up with them the next day. The rest of the time you can feel free to go home and sit quietly with no guilt or sense of lost opportunity. You may find, as your introvert author did, that you end up making some true, long-lasting and deep connections from this technique, sometimes more so than your more popular extrovert colleagues.

Another technique is to find your pair professionally. Have you got a colleague who is much more extrovert than you that you could swap advice with? Often the extroverts are genuinely too busy making connections with people to make advances in the work. Try a pair pact. You help them, they will help you. As the great Carl Jung pointed out: 'The meeting of two personalities is like the contact of two chemical substances. If there is any reaction, both are transformed.'

CUTTING THROUGH STRATEGY 4

Shhhh: cutting through as an introvert

On the way up

It is not easy to cut through when you are an introvert. Try looking at the problem from a professional problem-solving angle rather than as a personal issue. What techniques could you apply to the situation? If your bosses are all extrovert, can you suggest introducing coaching in personality profiles and diversity, as Marianne did? Can you form a pact with an extrovert colleague: you help them, they help you? Do a deal with yourself to work at networking or public speaking a couple of times a month in return for letting yourself off the hook the rest of the time.

From the top

We can only hope that extrovert bosses will read this paragraph. If all your appointments are extroverts, then you are missing out whatever your business is. Without introverts in the world we would be missing Van Gogh's *Sunflowers*, the theory of relativity and Apple. Your business needs both types and not just in the back room. Make your introverted talent feel as much a part of the business as the louder, attention-seeking extroverts. If you are an extrovert yourself, get yourself a truth-telling introvert partner at work. There is no actual sign that in business the meek will inherit, but they may well steal a competitive edge that you both need and want in your business.

Managing up – and sideways (that's your job too)

When one of us once got asked if they'd like to apply for a new job, the brief made us stop and think.

The job seemed interesting, and the company had a good reputation, so we asked for the candidate briefing. There were the usual requirements of experience, capabilities and what-have-you. There was also a paragraph that described their way of working as a 'Matrix-based collegiate system of shared values and aims'. Confused as to whether this meant that they were die-hard fans of science fiction films (and long leather coats), we enquired of the headhunter what that sentence meant.

Apparently, it meant that you had to learn to work together and be nice to your peer group. This seems blindingly obvious if you're to be a successful team, but clearly it needs to be emphasised in certain environments.

Corporate cultures have a life of their own, and negotiating them can be tricky. Quite often we commit to joining a new organisation on the basis of less than a few hours' interaction and our gut feel of whether we think it would work. The reality of what we've really signed up to can be a surprise.

Nicky was really pleased with her new role and the bigger level of responsibility it would bring. She had a great rapport with her new boss and knew that she could do great work in her new job. She had a few one-to-one meetings with her direct reports before she joined and got a feeling that things weren't quite what she had been told, but she just assumed that it was unfamiliarity that was causing her disquiet.

Four weeks in to her new job, and she and two of her direct reports were preparing a plan that they would put to the board. It was a key new development, and she was eager to mark the start of her new job with a slick, well-thought-out action plan. What she hadn't bargained with was the hostility that existed between her new colleagues. Any decision was agonisingly drawn out, and there was a tense atmosphere. A subsequent meeting proved just as painful, and this time she was joined by a supplier she'd worked with before. At the end of the second meeting, he stayed behind and said to Nicky, 'What is going on here? It's like walking on eggshells!'

So she went to her boss and explained the situation. She asked if he was aware of the tension, and he said that it had always been characterised to him as 'an appropriate dose of banter'. Nicky assured him it wasn't that, it was something far deeper, and she proposed her plan. Her predecessor had been a fully paid-up member of the 'divide and conquer' school of management, playing people off against each other and having different favourites at different times. Her two direct reports had got used to this and hadn't adjusted to the new way of working – perhaps hoping that finally one of them would gain the top spot. So Nicky deployed her plan and told both of them that they had a choice: to work together co-operatively or to leave. She got a coach in to facilitate the process, and it improved the situation massively. 'They will never go on holiday together, but at least they get the job done,' said Nicky afterwards.

Managing upwards is the key to keeping you and your career in the focus of your boss. This needn't be a thirty-minute outpouring face to face each week. It can be a brief email updating on progress on a project, a request for some feedback on some work in progress or just a cup of tea at the end of a period when you haven't had a catch-up. You don't have to fill the time with endless updates of your work in progress (this isn't therapy) – what you should aim to do is give them what they need to know and what you need from them.

With colleagues, there is little point in moaning that someone never circulates the meeting notes quickly enough. Swap tasks with them if it bothers you that much. Working with them to find the best way of working effectively is the way to set the wheels in motion.

CUTTING THROUGH STRATEGY 5

Managing up – and sideways (that's your job too)

On the way up

First of all, if you're expecting brilliant management from your boss, then think again. Great people management is rare. Consider yourself lucky if you have it. You will need to manage your boss – their expectations and their little ways. If you have a problem, don't moan about it: fix it, and then explain how you have fixed it. Don't take them problems; take them solutions. You also need to manage your peers. The crucial skill needed in getting the career you deserve is taking ownership of everything that you can find a way to fix. That means how you relate to people on your level who are not going to do what they are asked.

From the top

Here's the thing. Just because a subordinate is good at managing you, and perhaps flattering you, it doesn't necessarily make them good. Look out for yes-men and -women. And look out for those who need an explanation that you can't read their minds: if they want you to fix something, they need to spell it out.

CASE STUDY 6

Don't be a doormat

'No man is an island' is a well-known quotation, but, rather like your extended family, your colleagues are not necessarily people you would choose to spend your days with. Finding ways to work together or even co-existing without recourse to violence can sometimes seem a bit of a chore.

There is a fine line between finding a balance of being accommodating and finding common ground or just giving in at the first sign of conflict. It may feel that you are making things easier that way, but the truth is that you may just be a bit too passive for your own good.

Ellie is ambitious and self-aware, and she knows that success is based on having happy clients. She's not comfortable with aggression and in the early part of her career was in a culture that was, in her words, a 'bit too chest-beating hairy-gorilla macho' for her. She got a job at a company where she'd be working in a more thoughtful and ideas-driven environment. Ellie was conscious that her colleagues knew about the culture of her previous employer, so she worked hard to combat any notion that she was like that. What she hadn't realised was that her new colleagues needed her to push back on their behalf.

Ellie thought that by accommodating her clients' ideas, she was showing that she understood what they wanted to do. Even if she'd spent a week working on one of the initiatives they'd set her, she'd ditch the work without question if the client suggested another angle. After all, she was meant to keep the client happy ...

Eventually, another contact at her client asked her out for a drink. She told Ellie that she was in danger of losing the respect of both her main client and her colleagues. 'You never stand up for your ideas, you never make the case for all the work you do.' She told her that all of her ideas were becoming devalued because she was so accommodating.

Ellie took stock of what she had said and saw that she was right. She was working endlessly on projects that never got agreed or actioned. So were her colleagues.

The next week she sat down with her team and talked through how they were going to handle the client. Obviously a complete change in approach would be strange, so they planned how they'd deal with the next few meetings, who would talk about the work that they'd done and how they would handle client questions and suggestions.

We've all known people who think that their ideas or ways of working are the only ones that are right and will argue the case even in the face of logic. It's their way or no way. These people will either learn to work within the culture or run the risk of being seen as irrelevant (unless they are the boss, but that's a whole other story). Then there are the people – usually women – who just do whatever is needed or asked because the customer (or their boss) is always right. There is a healthy balance between these two extremes. You don't have to win every discussion, but neither do you need to just blindly work yourself into a frenzy if it's not the right thing to do. If you know your field, and the work that you can do, then you can argue from an informed point of view. Pick your fights and no-go areas, and be prepared to defend them.

CUTTING THROUGH STRATEGY 6

Don't be a doormat

On the way up

Listen to your instincts. If work is not progressing but you find yourself repeating the same effort over and over again, then just stop. Reassess what is going on, and be true to yourself.

From the top

Management consultant Pete Drucker said, 'There is no decision without disagreement.' Allow new ways of working and a change of approach as part of the work culture or be doomed to Groundhog Day.

CASE STUDY 7

Be seen

No one's career is a smooth upward, unhindered trajectory. How you deal with a tricky patch is crucial to your progress. Many women have a tendency to fade into the background when they hit a troublesome spot. As Sharon found, this is exactly the opposite of what you should do.

Sharon left Harvard Business School in the 1990s with top

qualifications. Her career has always been based in her city of birth, New York. Throughout that time her ambition has driven her to aspire for top jobs. More than once she's been told by her mainly male bosses to tone down her outspokenness. 'When Sheryl Sandberg at Facebook gives a talk she often uses the line "Hands up if you were ever told that you were too aggressive at work." Women raise their hand, men don't. That hasn't changed.'

She worries about motivational speeches to young women at conferences. She believes that the odds are still stacked against women, but that it is now unacceptable to talk about this because it is not politically correct. 'They tell women starting out, "You can be anything you want to be." Well, I think that this is the modern equivalent of the fairy godmother myth in Cinderella. We tell young women that the traditional companies where the management is a boys' club are dead and buried. Well, they aren't.'

Sharon thinks that, unless women are taught to understand the rules of the game, which are still largely dictated by men, then they can't win the game either by playing by the rules or by breaking them. In her recent, pessimistic experience the game has got tougher.

She was doing well in her new C-suite job in a growing business. Then a new boss arrived. She got on fine with him on the face of things. He appreciated her experience and professionalism. But gradually she became conscious that he wasn't inviting her to crucial meetings that she had been involved in under her previous boss. As she started to notice this, she started to become more sensitive to it. She began to question her importance to the business.

Eventually she came to the conclusion that, although her new boss said all the right things as far as women in business were concerned, he was, deep down, wired differently. 'He's lived in New York for over a decade. But he's in his forties. He grew up in a part of the world where he experienced a level of deference from women that, because I was brought up in the States, I have never come across. This makes a difference. Deep down a massive difference.'

As business becomes more global and fluid, women who have grown up in the so-called WEIRD (Western, Educated, Industrialised, Rich and Democratic) nations are going to come across more and more businessmen who have grown up in societies where the behaviour of men and women is culturally very different. No one is talking about this. In non-WEIRD nations society pays little attention to what women need. If this cultural accident happens to you, though, it is a real issue and needs highlighting, and facing. If you've grown up in one of the WEIRD countries as a woman, you're lucky. Even if it doesn't always feel like it.

So Sharon, who was the highly educated product of a WEIRD nation, had to deal with her alpha-male boss, who came from a very different culture. Even with her great job title and her fabulous reputation she found this very difficult. Her first response was to fade into the background completely. She stopped fighting to be included in big meetings and stopped speaking her mind when she was included.

'I just wasn't myself and I was less effective as a result.' Then something quite brilliant happened. Sharon goes on: 'My boss has a very tuned-in assistant. When I started at the company, I had a corner desk by a window. It was very nice, but it was tucked away, and I wasn't very visible. A spot opened up right next to the boss. His assistant came over to me and said, "You ARE moving there." I didn't want to, actually, but he made me. And it has made an enormous difference. You must not hide, you must not fade away. What was needed was for my boss to get used to me, to acclimatise to my persona. Now that we're "accidentally" together much more of the time, he has got used to me, and I can't tone myself down all the time so I am back to being myself, and all the more effective for it.'

Sharon's boss has now become acclimatised to her. He may not take her for a drink every night, but he does occasionally, without it being a big deal, and he feels comfortable. He can get the best out of her, and she can be herself with him.

Sharon had begun to be demoralised by her new boss. She felt overlooked, and she was allowing that to affect how she operated. A simple office move, away from her niche position in the corner, out into the open where she was highly visible, made all the difference.

CUTTING THROUGH STRATEGY 7

Be seen

On the way up

Sharon's new boss expected her to fade into the background, and she was beginning to comply. Don't let this happen. Don't be undermined. Make sure that you and your good work are visible. Sit where you will be noticed, and make sure that you amplify your achievements. If this feels immodest, or boastful, try ensuring that you include compliments to your team and to your boss as you do so. This will be more effective on every level.

From the top

A new culture can take a while to adapt to. If you are para-chuted into a new top job, you need to find a leadership persona that ensures that you get the best out of all of the talent, even if they are not your type. Spend more time with the ones that you are less inclined to spend time with. It will pay off.

Cutting Through in summary

Project 28–40 – The Report was first published by Opportunity Now, who campaign on gender diversity. It was designed by Business in the Community to act as a reality check for employers in 2014 to explore what the public really think about the gender pay gap and transparent reporting. The findings of the survey of 25,000 UK businessmen and -women were that there is a gap between organisational policies and the actual experiences of women aged between twenty-eight and forty. Most employees believe that there is a gender pay gap in their organisation, and think that employers should publish not only their overall gender pay gap but also pay data broken down by grade and job type. These years are obviously a time of change in the experience of some women, as they are the years when they may choose to have children. But it is also the point in a career when simply being good at what you do is no longer enough to ensure your next promotion. Mainly at this point anyone who is not any good at the job has been found out and moved on. So the place is full of people who can do the job well. The trick now is to stand out, to cut through the competition. Too many women shy away from this, as they lack the confidence or think that it is not in their nature. Either way it is necessary to learn how to cut through in order to achieve the career success that you deserve, and if you adopt the strategies summarised here, you will be pleased with the results.

Cutting Through: The strategies in brief

On the way up

1. Build your own personal brand. Work out the right image for you and then look, sound and act the part.

2. Speak their language. If you're proposing an idea, work out the best way to communicate it, even if that means 'speaking football'.

3. Be funny. Use humour to lighten the atmosphere. Store up a selection of jokes and deploy them at will. Too much seriousness implies a lack of confidence.

4. Cutting through as an introvert requires hard work. You do not need to take a huge leap out of your comfort zone, but you will need to find a way to extend it on your own terms.

5. Manage upwards and across. This is your responsibility too.

6. Stand up for your ideas. Don't allow the need to be liked to prevent you from being effective.

7. Be seen. Make sure that you are visible.

From the top

1. Watch out for hard-working team members who need training or coaching in standing out.

2. Make time and space for people who are suggesting new ideas to you. It may feel like an interruption of the working day, but you must be open to their ideas and understand that they won't necessarily speak your language.

3. Don't have different rules for different people as far as funny is concerned. Don't allow the banter in the workplace to squeeze anyone into a corner.

4. Make sure that your introverted team members receive the right level of respect and attention as the louder extroverts demand.

5. Give your team clarity on your expectations of being

managed as their boss. If their expectations of you and your all-knowingness are too high, then explain what they can expect and what you need from them.

6. Ensure that your whole team is expressing their real opinion. If everyone does as they are told all the time, then there is something wrong. It is all too easy to surround yourself with yes-men. It won't do you or the organisation any good in the long run.

7. Be sensitive to the different expectations of your team members, and spend time with the ones you just don't 'get' instinctively. It will pay off.

ONE VOICE: MERCEDES

Mercedes is in her mid-forties, happily married with no children. She has a high-powered job in the heart of the City of London. She's highly successful, she truly has cut through in the office so far, yet she is now considering the 'third leg of her career' as she has noticed that there is a conformist nature to the very senior jobs and that the very charac-teristics that have enabled her to stand out so far may begin to inhibit her career advance.

'I am forty-six years old. I started working in the fashion industry in Toronto. That was my first job. I found myself reading the business papers and wondering, why is this? Why is this? And just not under-standing so many aspects of what I was reading, and which I thought were probably very important. I felt as though I had one hand tied behind my back. Not sure I want to be in fashion for the rest of my life. There are a few other things I would like to learn. Why don't I take this opportunity to get my MBA? I sold everything, got a giant loan and went to business school in London.

'I ended up going into finance. Definitely somewhere I never thought I would actually be able to work. It was just for a summer job, but I had a great time, and they asked me if I wanted to stay. They hired me for when I finished business school. That's how I ended up there.

'And now I'm at the point where no one intimidates me. And it isn't possible to be bored. There are so many smart people there and there's so much stuff to do. And there are another five jobs over there that I haven't got a clue about yet, and the learning curve would be massive if I went to go and do one of them. I feel like I have a lot more that I would like to learn and probably share, and build upon.

'Private wealth management in London is not as easy for someone like me, who is essentially still an outsider, in that a lot of wealth in England is hunting, shooting and fishing. It is not that obvious at the beginning, but you know you have to have a social edge.

'I think they would be shocked if I said to the guy behind me, "I will try this shooting business out. I am sure I could get an invitation." They would just be shocked that I actually would want to do that.

'I am just not interested in it. Standing in the rain shooting birds. I don't know. I definitely don't want to ever shoot a deer.

'There are parts of the job where your edge is fluidity in that social stratosphere.

'One of the most heated conversations we can have at work is the fact that among my team – that's twelve people, about four women – no one has a wife that works.

'I asked one of them, "Why doesn't your wife work? Doesn't she want to?" (I am friends with her too.) He replied, "You know because she has her art thing she wants to do – she finds it very satisfying." I replied, "Well, we go to the Cayman Islands for the last two weeks of August every year, and I find that really satisfying. But I can take as many pictures as I want; my mortgage company is not going to take that as payment."

'I just feel, why would you do this to yourself? Yet people feel very secure in that kind of arrangement, not having a profession. I would not. I always want my independence.

'We had a heated debate about this with some friends over the weekend. My friend felt offended because she felt that her mother was unable to work outside the home when her kids were young (she was a farmer's wife). But I said, "I don't want you to be offended. I am not trying to say, your mother was bad because she didn't have a job. But if I had a daughter, I couldn't tell her, it would be OK." None of the directors' wives work, you know.

'I think, they don't look at me any differently from them. You know, one of the team of the guys. They might look at me differently from their wife.

'I have so many single friends. And some of that is born out of the fact that we don't have children. You know your social life gets moulded by your circumstances as well.

'It just kind of happened. When I got married, having kids never even crossed my mind for years. I think that was because my husband and I both started pretty much from zero when we graduated from business school. Ambitious, and in debt. I just thought, well I haven't done all this to just be poor, and to have to pay for childcare and not live in the apartment I want to live in. And not do what I want to do. I would see people at work, and women would say, "I have got to leave because my husband is travelling on business and I have to get home for the nanny." I'd say, "Why have you got to leave? He was travelling last week. Why are you always the default partner?" I find that scary. I would say to my husband, if we have kids, are you going to be working part-time? Are you going to take Fridays off? Well, if the answer were no, then I don't want to do it either.

'I don't know, maybe it would be different. I assume when you have a baby it's different. But I just feel that I would just be pissed off. You know when is he getting home? You know I am home, I've come home. What time is he getting here? I can't leave the house, but where is he? I know he is at a meeting, but I have left my meeting. Could we get through it? The pressure on our marriage and our situation? We get on so well, we have so much fun, it's easy to text from the pub at eight and say, "Oh I am still out for drinks, I will be home around nine."'

'Having kids would be a pressure on our situation.

'We may still do it. When we talk about it, these are the sorts of thing that we always talk about: who's ready to be the person that leaves work early? Can I really get assurance that if I did it last time, you'd do it this time?

'I don't want to hear him say that his meeting is more important, because my needs are important too.'

CHAPTER 4

TROUBLE

*Trouble troubles women differently
from how it troubles men*

Conventional wisdom has it that women are too self-effac-
ing in the workplace. They work away in the shadows
and never say boo to a goose. If only they got themselves
noticed, then everything would be OK. They just need to speak
up, be more prominent and believe in themselves. For most
women, most of the time, that's probably true; in this book we
offer plenty of advice on stepping up and being seen. But then
it is probably true for many men as well. Man or woman – it
doesn't get you anywhere to be continually overlooked.

Yet both men and women need to balance attention-seeking with a genuine self-awareness.

As this chapter shows, if you're combative without
substance, if you believe in your own publicity a bit too
much or if you put too much of your faith in a vague notion
of fairness at work, then you can expect to get your come-
uppance in one way or another.

The Ancient Greeks called this kind of trouble meeting
your Nemesis. Nemesis was the Greek goddess of divine retribution, specifically targeted against those who provoked her
by hubris or arrogance. As we will see in our case studies, if
you use your sexuality to attract attention to yourself, then

you really need to be careful. Nemesis loves to strike and, yes, unfair as it seems, she strikes more cruelly at women.

However, a visit from Nemesis might teach a valuable lesson, and could be a springboard to the next stage of your career, or even to a new employer who will truly appreciate you for who you are and what you can contribute. So when Nemesis strikes and bad things appear to happen, it can be the start of something really positive.

We all respond differently to difficulties in the workplace. The key is to keep everything in perspective and remember that there is something to be learned in every experience. Often we can feel so alone, so isolated when trouble hits us. Our inspirational role models sometimes airbrush stories about their career progression that make them look small or in the wrong. These are *exactly* the stories we need them to tell us, because feeling alone in a storm is not exactly great encouragement for bravery or resilience. When you read this chapter, you'll learn that, however bad your experience has been, there is definitely a precedent; and even if the details of what has happened to you are not in these pages, then perhaps a similarity will encourage you to pick yourself up and get through the storm.

Do you know the AA prayer which they recite at meetings? 'God, grant me the serenity to accept the things I cannot change, the courage to change the things I can, and the wisdom to know the difference.' We're not proposing prayer as a resource when trouble strikes, but a good sense of when to fight back and when to flee is essential to building a career. If there's never any discord in your working life, then you may be holding back. We don't suggest you court trouble, but we will show you how to deal with it.

Keep going

It is the review from Hell. It's a Monday morning. It's about 11 a.m. Jools enters her boss Gavin's office nervously. It is time for her annual performance review. Gavin is leaning back in his office chair, crotch thrust forward, slightly reeking of his cycle ride into work. The atmosphere stinks – in more ways than one. Behind her, Dave, a recently promoted colleague, slinks in too.

'I thought I'd invite Dave to join us, Jools,' says Gavin. 'You see, I thought his presence would make things smoother.' Jools smothers a complaint. For the last year Dave and Jools have been on the same level, and while Dave has just been promoted, Jools doesn't report in to him, and has no intention of doing so. But this session is likely to be a difficult one anyway – better to save the push-back for when it is needed.

The review begins. It is surprisingly good. Jools knows Gavin doesn't like her. And she knows why. But as she is excellent and inventive at what she does, Gavin has had to acknowledge this in the first three-quarters of the report, which are task-based scores of competency. Jools starts to relax, despite the posturing and lack of fresh air.

They reach the final page of the report. This is the section left free for Gavin's comments. Once they've finished running through the review, it goes into Jools's permanent record and directly affects her chances of a promotion and pay rise. 'I'll just let you read through what I've written,' says Gavin. Dave so far hasn't (perhaps wisely) opened his mouth. As Jools reads the report, her restraint snaps. After three pages of a consistently great performance review Gavin has written: 'Although Jools's ability is clear, she is sometimes destructive and disruptive.'

Jools takes a deep breath. She waits a beat. She says: 'I don't think you have any idea, Gavin, of just how destructive and disruptive I have the potential to be.'

At this point Dave intervenes. He too is seeing the report for the first time, and he's fond of Jools. 'I think this is a bit much, Gav … perhaps you should tone it down a bit.'

There and then Gavin reaches across to the delete button on his computer and starts to eradicate what he has written. 'I can't believe you're doing that,' says Jools to her boss, as she sweeps out. 'If you have the cheek to come up with that in the first place, you should at least have the courage to justify it, and to stick with it.'

How did the situation get this bad, and what should Jools have done about it?

There was a laddishness about this office environment that tends to permeate organisations with only a few senior women.

Gavin was one of the bosses at the agency's media department. From New Zealand originally, he was a lover of practical jokes. In particular, he enjoyed setting off bangers, and ordered them especially from France, where they made them louder.

When Jools joined the department, as one of the youngest women in the team, she sat opposite Thomas, a gentle man in his fifties of a nervous disposition. Behind the desks runs a balcony. Gavin regularly hides on the balcony in order to suddenly explode a banger to make Thomas jump. Thomas does jump. He jumps out of his skin. After just a few occasions of tolerating Gavin's pranks, Jools corners her boss in the bar one night. This is the office bar, but it's not the office. She therefore feels perfectly justified in bluntly suggesting that Gavin stops with the bangers. She may even have suggested that this kind of behaviour wasn't very professional, wasn't exactly helpful to Thomas's health, and that if you enquired of the clients whether this was behaviour that they'd be willing to pay for, then the answer would be in the negative.

This interaction is enough to finish any relationship that might ever have existed between the two of them. Gavin didn't choose to have Jools in his team. Her previous boss had left for another job, and Gavin had made a play for his accounts, which meant that he got Jools too. Gavin could not believe the level of disrespect that Jools was showing. Jools couldn't believe the level of disrespect that he was showing not only her but the whole team (particularly lovely, nervous Thomas).

Shortly afterwards came the performance review. Shortly after that Jools did what she should have done much sooner. She called a headhunter, got another job and in fact achieved a significant pay rise by moving, partly because she had been under-promoted where she was.

Her male boss had felt undermined by her challenge for some time and continually passed over her. She moved to work for one of the few (she could count them on one hand) women bosses in her industry, who welcomed her with open arms and a BMW company car.

What would have happened if this testosterone-laden confrontation had never taken place? Would Jools have lingered unrewarded for longer? Would she have assumed that she didn't deserve better and allowed her confidence to be undermined even more?

Sometimes, as difficult as this can be to accept, it is much better to make things worse, so that you can see clearly what you should do.

There are some situations that you just should not put up with. How confrontational you decide to be about them is a personal matter, but it is essential to exude an air of confidence to others in the workplace who are undermining your position. It should say: 'Don't even go there.'

What about Gavin? He ended up losing a key useful staff member. If he'd tried to understand how she was different from the rest of the team, not just physically but in style and personality, then he might have kept her. Gavin clearly could not have cared less, but his boss did, and when Jools resigned his boss held him responsible. Not long afterwards he relocated back to New Zealand. He missed the point of management: that sometimes you just don't get the response that you plan for. He didn't think things through, and he didn't understand that talented people will often react differently from your expectations – they're going to challenge you and either you can handle that or they will leave, leaving you with a pack of yes-men.

In the story above, Jools had provoked Gavin, and Nemesis struck in the shape of a very personal, and potentially harmful, performance review. Unpleasant though this was, the setback was actually a springboard. It was time for her to re-set her career by a change of workplace and a new job that had the potential to be the launch pad for real and lasting success.

If Jools had accepted the original review as it was intended, and if she had allowed the unfair criticism to stand, then she would have muddled on for longer and failed to grasp the opportunity that was within her reach. Jools was entitled to challenge the pranks her boss insisted on in the workplace. When that challenge had disproportionate consequences, her only practical alternative was not to back down but to get out of there.

Keep going

On the way up

If you get yourself into trouble, keep going. Jools didn't put the brakes on, she accelerated. This brought matters to a head, and ultimately set her free from a damaging situation. She should perhaps have seen this coming, but her confidence had been undermined over time. A chat with a mentor would have set her straight. Find a mentor, outside the business, and use them.

From the top

If you treat good people like this, you're going to lose them. If there is a homogeneous culture in your company that doesn't even tolerate exceptions, let alone value them, then what do you expect is going to happen? A good manager will ensure that everyone who is valuable in their team feels welcome.

CASE STUDY 2

Is sex a problem?

Sexuality confuses the workplace. Flirting and banter can be tricky to navigate. In a traditionally male-populated environment, where most of the jobs are held by men, or where all of the high-status jobs are held by men, the atmosphere is going to be different from one where there's a more equal gender mix. In this case even one senior woman can make the difference. To this day many women daily navigate a barrack-room atmosphere that diverts their valuable time and energy away from their careers. Naturally there are talented men, too, who are alienated by this culture.

Gill, now director of a business based in Silicon Valley, recalls her first job working for an auditing company in Britain. Everyone in senior positions was male. They always had been. There was a culture of the senior men sleeping with junior women. In her early twenties, glamorous and fiercely intelligent, it was standard for her to be greeted with remarks like this on an average cold winter's day: 'You could dial a phone with those nipples.' When she walked out to pitch for business, her colleagues' idea of encouragement was to shout, 'Remember, Teeth, Tits and Arse!'

Sitting and recalling these days, just over a decade ago, we are all shocked at some of her memories, including once being patted on the bottom. 'I didn't think it was that bad to be honest at the time; it was called "banter" and I was used to it from my rugby friends at university.'

Nowadays that kind of behaviour would be unthinkable, or at least we hope so. Gill puts it down to the fact that there had never been a woman with any kind of seniority at the firm, and maintains that she knew that they respected her intelligence and in fact admired her. 'In some ways I gave as good as I got.'

If only inappropriate behaviour was completely consigned to history. Another of our interviewees (now MD of her business) told a recent story of an experience with a senior colleague when he visited her, when she was working in a more junior role, in Sydney. He would pop up every three months or so in order to keep her updated with the latest developments. She was consistently flattered by how he paid attention to her opinions and made time for her. On the last visit the meeting ran late, he offered dinner (with others), then offered to share her cab home – she could drop him at his hotel. When they stopped, he suggested a last drink. Should she have gone straight home? Maybe, but would a man in her position have had to consider the wisdom of stopping at the bar for a drink with his boss? His boss who had made no intimate overtures ever in any previous encounter? When the bar was very busy, with no free seats, and he suggested a drink in his room instead should she have fled? Maybe, but she felt as though this would massively insult him. Perhaps you can guess the rest. When he shut the hotel bedroom door behind him and shoved her instantly on to the bed, she pushed him off and fled. What was he thinking? This is not 'mixed signals'; this is inappropriate behaviour in a boss.

If that's just one example that we can identify with, at least it is clearly something that everyone knows how react to. No ambiguity there. More common are low levels of everyday, should-we-call-it-sexism-or-not, instances in the office. The times when the team, who are all blokes apart from you, banter about meeting a new colleague or client. They'll reference that she is 'up for it', talk about her physical appearance in a way that embarrasses you, frankly verges on the soft end of pornography. If you object, are you making too big a deal about it? Are you failing to take it light-heartedly enough? Surely you can't call them on it every time?

Of course, you must make a judgement, but in our view, as we've said, this is fundamentally about the culture of your company, or of your team. A good business culture will make sure that everyone feels welcome and strive to get the best out of individual talent. If you don't say anything, that culture will not emerge in your office. So whether you choose to banter back in a way that ensures that you get your point across, or whether you choose to take senior management aside and explain to them what they're failing to improve, you can, and indeed should, make your feelings clear.

Is sex a problem?

On the way up

If you don't like the tone of the banter around you, do something about it. Giving as good as you get is one first step. Why not give even more than you get – don't let anyone get away with undermining your professionalism, even for a moment. Work out a powerful, preferably witty, response and continually deliver it, at even the slightest sign of inappropriate behaviour. If the banter is public, make sure your put-down is public too. Don't let them get away with it. You won't get any benefit from sounding like a nun in the locker room. You will win with a bit of well-rehearsed and well-aimed wit. If the inappropriateness escalates, then escalate the situation to the highest possible level. Make sure that everyone is clear that this is unacceptable behaviour. Too often women don't want to make a fuss. Make a fuss. You're doing this not just for yourself but for any other woman who might find themselves in the same position. You will get support.

From the top

If you're the boss and you're tolerating this kind of atmosphere in the workplace and then wondering why you don't have senior women in the team, then you need to wake up and smell the coffee. We know of one male-dominated sales team where everyone is asked, on a Monday morning, how much sex they had over the weekend. Surprise surprise, they've never ever developed a senior woman in that team. The business notionally nods to diversity, and they deal with women at a senior level as customers, so it is an embarrassment never to be able to field them in a meeting on their side of the table. They've had to pay over the odds to employ women in senior roles, and then they don't stay long. This really isn't hard to diagnose, and it's not rocket science to solve. Try asking instead about where the team went for dinner not whom they went to bed with.

Sex in the office

Gill goes on to tell us a story of a woman at her subsequent job who had slept with several men in the company. Someone decided it would be funny to create a Powerpoint presentation of all the men she'd slept with, and a candidate list of who was next. This was circulated to all staff. Although this organisation was larger, and had a culture of what was and was not acceptable in terms of public banter, there was still a sense that this individual, because she was a woman with multiple sexual partners, had somehow brought this exposure on herself. She deserved her Nemesis.

Simon, who now runs his own consultancy, spent years in male-run, macho-spirited companies. His view is clear. Blokes get away with it, and women don't. He says, 'Unfortunately there are a number of behaviours in the workplace that I personally find appalling, and sadly they still exist. As a woman, you'll undermine yourself ten times more. A male MD might have slept with everyone in the company and that's OK, but that woman sitting there – it's a different set of rules. I think it is a big mistake for a bloke, too, from a personal point of view, but it is not as big a career mistake. As a woman, you're giving someone tools to hurt you.'

Eventually this culture may change, but at the moment there's a double standard. Pragmatism is the first step. Do not make the mistake of thinking that the double standard won't affect you because it isn't fair.

The deeper consequences of sex in the office seem to be not much more than embarrassment.

Everyone enjoys a good gossip; the prevailing mood in offices these days is let he who is without sin throw the first stone. However, only an idiot expects to gain any career benefit from sex. The days of building a career on the casting couch are long over.

Sue Douglas, one of the first female newspaper editors in the UK, recounts her most acutely embarrassing brush with a sex scandal. Her friend the writer Julie Burchill featured her in a novel barely disguised as young, gorgeous, sensuous Susan Street, who 'is not satisfied with being deputy editor of the newspaper. She wants it all, and she will do it all to fight her way to the top and fulfil her lust for ambition.'

Ambition, published in 1990, recreated specifically something that Sue Douglas had lived through, as the book opens with a scene where the protagonist finds herself alone in a bed with her boss, her married boss, who has just died of a heart attack. We won't spoil the plot of a book that Burchill says 'makes *Fifty Shades of Grey* seem like *Anne of Green Gables*'.

As you can imagine, finding herself quite that notorious was a shock for Douglas at the time. Her response to the situation? 'Mentally roll up your sleeves. Always remember that you do know what you're doing, so you can deal with it.'

Sex in the office

On the way up

What's the best tactic? JDDI: Just Don't Do It. However, if you do do something you wish could stay private and doesn't, brazen it out and be grateful that it probably won't be revealed in a best-selling novel. If people know it's you, then don't be afraid to talk about yourself; get your story out there too. In that situation it won't hurt to actually say to people, 'Hey, have you heard what happened to me?' You'll get points for honesty if nothing else. If they don't know who, what, when or even that it's you, then deny any knowledge.

From the top

In this situation you stand by your talented team member. You say, 'This is her private life, and I think it's entirely up to her what she does with it.' But give her this chapter to read.

The Conspiracy of the Sisterhood: kindness can kill

During our careers we're always delighted when we find a kindred spirit, someone whom you can celebrate and commiserate with and who gets where you are coming from as well as where you're going to. Yet in our experience there is helpful help and unhelpful help. This is what we shall refer to as The Conspiracy of the Sisterhood.

The Conspiracy of the Sisterhood isn't malicious or premeditated. In fact, the perpetrators would be horrified to be seen as anything other than supportive, involved and helpful. Yet they might end up in a special place in hell too, despite their best intentions. As the saying goes, the road to hell is paved with good intentions. It is the good intentions that make it much worse when you are confronted with The Conspiracy of the Sisterhood, as we shall see in this experience.

Sally and Lucy worked together early in their careers and had found a kindred spirit in each other. It was a blessing to have a friend at work who knew what you were going through, a colleague who could be trusted to share your views on how things could be done better and someone who had your back. They both progressed up through the company side by side, though careful to be seen as separate entities. In time, Lucy left to join another organisation that offered a quicker route to the top, and although it was a risky move, Sally was supportive of Lucy's choice. Lucy was a huge success in her new role, and they were always in touch. A while later, Sally started a family, then returned to a bigger role after her maternity leave.

This is where we encounter one instance of the Conspiracy. Coming back to a new role, with more to do and a bigger stake in the future of the company is a challenge. Doing it post-maternity leave is an even bigger ask. You've changed, your role has changed, you want to grasp the opportunity, but you're not 100 per cent certain of your path any more. So Sally turned to her friend for advice. After all, Sally had always found Lucy the best source of practical guidance, with a realistic take on situations.

Lucy was eager to share her experiences. Over cups of coffee and glasses of wine they discussed Sally's situation. Knowing Sally well, she was confident that she could help. Lucy had been there, done that and wanted Sally to blossom in the new role. She had a lot to share. She had a lot of very good advice. She knew exactly what Sally needed to do and the behaviour that she needed to adopt. Leaning in, working hard, learning new skills, networking more were all part of the advice she gave. There was just one problem. All of this made Sally feel worse than ever.

Lucy and Sally weren't in the same company any more. Their roles were different too.

Their home lives were different. The idea of networking a certain number of nights a week just wasn't possible for Sally. Taking time out after her maternity leave to do a course wasn't practical either.

So Lucy's advice felt dissonant, and Sally felt conflicted. Her friend was a big success, celebrated and admired. How can it be that what she said didn't feel right? That the pep talks don't push you on, the reassurance isn't there? It always did the job in the past. Maybe it's you. You don't get it any more. You feel off-centre, disorientated and confused. Is it possible that you are a bit stupid?

The fact is that your paths have diverged. All you have in common is a shared past.

The company Lucy had worked for is still there, but it has changed, and so has the work and so have the people. Where Lucy now works is not the same, even if it's in the same area of business – the values, culture and needs are distinct.

So Sally finds herself in turmoil: whom do you talk to when the Sisterhood isn't working out for you? Does having no gut instinct make you gutless? And how is it that you got this far up until now, and suddenly you are unsure and equivocating? The Conspiracy of the Sisterhood is Nemesis because, in career terms, kindness can kill. It makes it really hard to find your own voice and direction. The temptation to follow in the slipstream of another woman's career trajectory can be enormous. The problem is that this isn't really you pushing forward. You are behind someone else, and one day you are going to be on your own, with people looking at you for the answer or a direction, and it isn't a quiz show where you can phone a friend. If you follow in another person's slipstream, you will end up crashing.

The Conspiracy of the Sisterhood: kindness can kill

On the way up

If you need mentoring, find a mentor who has nothing to do with your past or even your present. It won't help you to change if you take advice from someone who knows the old you. Taking on a different or bigger role, particularly when your life has changed, requires huge energy. You need to fuel that energy, and you therefore need to be ruthless with regard to where you seek that fuel. An old friend or a close friend comes with all kinds of baggage. Sure, catch up with her over a coffee, but seek true helpful mentoring from someone objective.

One of our interviewees spoke about the idea of companies embracing the idea of 'sponsors' for women at work, people who actively promote your career, and you, at key points in your working life. There are personal experiences that change people and their needs. So companies who recognise that the response needs to be tailored to the individual, rather than a one-size-fits-all HR policy, can create immense loyalty among their teams. Recognition that, at some points, a gradual assumption of a new role is a required transition for colleagues to get a real grip of the task, rather than thinking that they can just do it, instantly from day one. Any new role requires an enormous amount of emotional and physical energy. Maternity isn't the only situation that this applies to. Elderly parents who are frail can be equally demanding of a colleague's time and emotional energy. It's a human trait to compare yourself to others. It's worth remembering that the things that fulfil you (families, volunteering, exercise) are rarely the same for other people. And that they may feel that you are better off (in any number of ways) than they are.

From the top

As a manager, look at your management techniques and adapt them so they are relevant to each individual. One size doesn't fit all, and the investment in people will pay back in abundance. Make sure people know that you're there to get the best from them and then DO IT.

CASE STUDY 5

Mean girls

It's a tough world out there, and for many women the prospect of working with a group of other women and reporting to a female boss after a long time in a male-dominated environment can seem like manna from heaven. No more hovering around the door of the men's toilets listening to conversations your male peer group have at the urinals in an attempt to keep you in the dark. No more being asked if you are someone's secretary because the company you work for has a reputation for not employing women.

Working for a woman, of course, is not an automatic panacea. When a woman shifts from a masculine culture to work for a woman, it can seem as though it will be. Of course it is not. If you work for someone who wants you to be a mini (not quite as good) clone, then you will find it frustrating, as Naomi's story shows.

After working at her job for over five years in a male-dominated organisation, Naomi was delighted to be headhunted out of her role for a bigger job and to work for a charming man who was going places and wanted to take her with him. It was a bonus that the company she joined had a tradition of senior women managers. Working for him was interesting and stimulating, and he encouraged her to develop her skills and build her profile. One thing he couldn't teach, though, was the political nature of where they worked, and after losing out on an internal promotion he left. Initially this looked like an opportunity for Naomi. There was a reorganisation that gave her a bigger role and which promoted her above her peers.

This change resulted in Naomi working for a new person, Paula. She was a woman who had a different skill set but who welcomed Naomi's experience and seemed eager to be supportive, engaged and, above all, friendly. Initially it all went well, and Naomi felt she was navigating the changes to her role in the way that her boss wanted. Her new boss was more analytical than her old one and had said that she found the current procedures a little slapdash and that she wanted much more reporting and analysis, so Naomi happily created more reports. Before every meeting with a new client or contact, long preparation notes were required for Paula to be able to comprehend how the relationship worked.

Gradually Naomi realised that this was taking up a disproportionate amount of her time. All of the qualities that Naomi felt she was promoted for – her natural intelligence, her flair and creativity, her networking skills – were seemingly being slowly squashed into a world of detail, internal meetings and endless analysis. It was analysis that was never used as a starting-point for a new approach or to inform subsequent actions. However, on the other hand, Paula could be fun on an informal level; she would suggest clothes Naomi might like or a new hairstyle. Naomi wasn't as much of a clothes horse as Paula and never acted on the suggestions – she just loved the glimpses into a life where you shopped at Jimmy Choo on a regular basis.

One day Naomi had a disagreement about a project with Ian, one of her direct reports.

She had been promoted above him, and he was very sensitive to any perceived challenge to his position or his authority, so she was careful with him and felt that they had reached a solution by the end of their talk. The following day she was called in by her boss, who informed Naomi that she had been approached by Ian, who had complained about the endless reporting and the over-analysis. It appeared that Paula had regularly been chatting to Ian about work and that he had shared his views with her. Naomi was astonished that her performance was the subject of cosy post-work chats and that she was being criticised for doing what Paula had asked her to do. She told Paula that this complaint hadn't been raised with her – that Ian had been annoyed when he wasn't the one promoted, and that he had made that clear to everyone. Paula said nothing in response.

This event started a new phase in their relationship, where Naomi received mixed signals from Paula. One day would end with them talking about their plans for the weekend and clothes shopping; the next week, Paula would tell Naomi not to ask personal questions if she said 'Good weekend?' on a Monday. Told off for putting her feet on the desk ('It is too casual and sets a bad example') during a two-hour call with a client at 7 p.m., Naomi started to feel that daily life in the office was like a bad dream. What was good work one week was bad work the next. Naomi felt that she never knew what reaction or reception she would get on a day-to-day basis.

In parallel there seemed to be a cluster of other women around Paula whom she had picked out and who were much more in her image.

Naomi convinced herself that, if she worked really hard, delivered on all of her projects and persisted, it would all come right in the end. Even if she wasn't blonde enough or wearing the right shoes, surely her work would redeem her?

So months passed and, feeling increasingly isolated, Naomi began to count down the hours until Friday night. Waking up at the weekend gradually lost its joy as she realised it was only two days until she would be walking on eggshells again, an ominous feeling compounded by her paranoia that her peer group were aware of the chasm between her and Paula.

In the end, driving to work on a sunny day, Naomi realised that this was no way to spend her career and that she needed to get out. But her self-esteem was nil, and she wasn't sure she could manage an interview for a paper round at the moment. She acted on impulse, and out of sheer misery. Seizing the moment, she asked to see Paula and told her of her intention to resign and that her formal letter would follow. Paula didn't want to accept her resignation and asked her to rethink – after all, Naomi was such a key team member, and Paula didn't think she could cope without her. Could Naomi sleep on it for twenty-four hours?

Imagine the turmoil of that twenty-four hours. Every attitude that had been drummed in to Naomi throughout her career was to work hard and earn a good living. Nobody just walks out of a job with no idea of what to do next, do they? However, twenty-four hours later Naomi handed in her letter of resignation, and four months after that she left the company. She had no job to go to, but she knew that if she stayed where she was, she would either be crushed or have become like everyone else in the gang.

This is the Mean Girls syndrome. There is one image and one way of working that a dominant female puts in place. Deviate, and it seems to defy her authority.

This situation could easily have happened to anyone, regardless of gender. You're not a football fan, but your boss wants a minimum five-minute chat about the game at the weekend (a colleague said he can never confess to not knowing the intricacies of the offside rule).

On the other hand, as a boss, your own personal preferences and approach should never cloud your judgement and dominate work to such an extent that you are either a dictator-like manager or seen as a prima donna. Chest-beating to prove who is in charge should never be encouraged as a way of taking people with you. You need to lead from the front, back and side to take your vision and your colleagues forward.

TROUBLE STRATEGY 5

Mean girls

On the way up

This strategy is really simple. Never deviate from your true self. Never, ever. You cannot succeed in an environment where you cannot be yourself. Time after time women try to conform so that they will fit in. Don't. The effort that it takes will distract from your ability to do good work and, at worst, it will totally undermine your self-confidence. Naomi ended up working somewhere great after only a brief period without a job. More importantly, she had learned a good (if painful) lesson from her experiences working for Paula. Now running a large company, she is one of the most authentic, inspiring and effective women we have encountered. Always be yourself.

From the top

As a business, regularly work on whether your company has an 'inclusive' culture that creates the environment for talent to shine, rather than employing the same old types and then expecting a different outcome.

CASE STUDY 6

Know when to back down

Like Naomi in the previous case study, sometimes you have to know when to back down after Nemesis has struck. The consequences of keeping going and sticking with your principles are just not worth it.

Jess was delighted to be part of the team that was on its way to see a prominent entrepreneurial business tycoon. She'd been brought into the team by her boss, the CEO, who had picked her out personally. Today they were due to go along and receive a brief from the tycoon. They had all been told in advance that he was notoriously short-tempered and keen to maintain that reputation.

To begin with, the tycoon – let's call him Sean – showed them around his company's stock room, explaining what a good deal he had done on every item, a much better deal than the people working for him could have managed.

'How many of these do you think we're selling?' he continually asked the team, and was delighted when they got the answers hopelessly wrong. It was as if he relished making them look a bit rubbish.

'These items weren't selling at all,' Sean proclaimed,

waving some goods in front of the team, 'so I told them to change the price point from three for two to 30 per cent off and they sold out. You,' he said pointing at Jess, 'You, what's the difference between three for two and 30 per cent off?'

This was where Jess made her first mistake. She answered the question as asked, and replied, 'Er ... 3 per cent.'

'Are you sure?' came the reply.

For a few moments Jess was not sure of anything, not even her own name, as Sean leaned forward in her face and pointed a stubby finger at her.

'Well, yes, it's 3 per cent,' she muttered sheepishly. (She could do mental arithmetic perfectly well, and three for two comes to 66.66 (recurring) per cent, and 30 per cent off comes to 70 per cent, and the difference is about 3 per cent, and well, you get the picture.)

Wrong (right) answer. Sean had wanted to make the point that there was hardly any difference. He felt that she was detracting from his point by giving a specific answer. It hardly mattered what she had said. She had got his attention, and now that he had her in his sights, he wasn't sure that he liked her.

They moved now to Sean's luxurious office. Here he talked for a while about how brilliant he was at his job, before turning to the CEO and asking him what his ideas were.

The CEO turned to Jess, the ideas woman. Now, strictly speaking, this was not supposed to be an ideas session. Remember the brief for this meeting was that the team were there to take a brief from Sean, not to give him ideas. But Jess had prepared rough thoughts for the session just in case. She was too experienced to be flummoxed by this change of direction.

She rolled out a couple of ideas. Sean considered them, dismissed one out of hand, quite liked the other one, but ended up dismissing it too as taking too long to deliver. 'Do you think I've got all year to sort this out?' he expostulated. 'It's not going to work quickly enough. You have not wowed me, you have not entertained me,' he ended angrily.

Here's Jess's second mistake. After all, there was nothing that would have made her shut up at this provocation – she's just not that type. She took a breath and said: 'Well, I didn't come here to wow you or to entertain you. I'm not an entertainer, I'm a business problem-solver. If you want to, we can now talk about your business problem from your perspective. If you don't want to, then perhaps I should get my coat?'

What was she thinking? Did she actually think that this challenge would cause a level of respect and a desire to hear more? If so, she was wrong. And she realised how wrong as she was, indeed, shown the door. She wept on the way home, as she felt that she had let her boss down badly. The truth is that the only way to respond in that situation would have been to respond humbly. This wasn't a business discussion at all; it was an alpha-male contest.

A reply such as 'I couldn't agree with you more' might have allowed her to stay in the room, and have given her a central role in a second meeting. She had been challenged to show some respect for the alpha male in the situation, and she had failed to do so. When she talked to her CEO about it sometime later, she was able to apologise to him for letting him down.

He brushed it off, saying that there were much bigger priorities for her to deliver than this.

He also said that he could see the whole thing coming as soon as they reached Sean's offices and were introduced. 'It was like a car crash in slow motion. I could see it coming, I couldn't think of anything to do or to say to stop it.'

Know when to back down

On the way up

Sometimes you need to back down and read the room. Don't lose your temper. Maintain equilibrium, and choose your moment to be smart. Being smart isn't always what's required. If you can't win the fight, it may be better to give way for now. Responding with a calm and considered reply agreeing with the bully spoiling for a fight isn't giving in, any more than a parent is giving in to a toddler having a tantrum when they try to distract them. If the bully is acting like a five-year-old, then you need to be the grown-up. Calmly, quietly, say: 'I definitely agree with you; now that you've pointed that out I can see how right you are. Now, how can my team help you with your dilemma?'

From the top

Jess's CEO might have accidentally landed her in it, but he handled the aftermath pretty well. He let her calm down, brushed off her apology and restored her confidence by giving her a task that she could handle. He can expect, and indeed deserves, her loyalty for the long term. He made it clear that he learned something from the situation as well.

CASE STUDY 7

The burnout

Linda had given her all to the major retail account that she worked on. It was the agency's largest account, and she had been given overall responsibility for keeping the client happy.

She relished the challenge and was determined not to let the board of the company down. For a while all went well. The account seemed to require her to work ten-hour days regularly and to accommodate meetings at the weekends, but she didn't mind. She was single, childless and at a life stage where she felt able to put her hand up for any challenge to further her career. After several months of gruelling workload it became clear that all was not OK. The senior client, a very driven woman, began to question the quality of the thinking on the account. Linda was putting so many hours in that it was difficult to see clearly, and she tried to improve the situation by working harder still. By the time she realised that she had to ask for help from her boss, she was very emotional and had lost perspective. As her confidence was undermined over a period of months she dug herself in, blamed herself more and gently disintegrated.

'This was my mistake,' she confided in us. 'You shouldn't ask for help when you are really upset. You have to be able to be clinical. I should have asked myself how I would feel if someone came to me in such an upset state.'

The help Linda received wasn't enough. She should probably have raised the possibility of coming off the account to her line manager. One of the reasons she did not do so was that she felt some connection to the senior client simply because they were both women. This was misguided. Linda had no more affinity with her than she would have done with a man. But it felt a bigger failure to Linda to have to ask to quit in this circumstance. So she felt too vulnerable to do so, and continued on the account as her life and health deteriorated. She just worked harder and harder. To be in a client meeting when your downstairs neighbour calls to say that a section of your floor has collapsed into the flat below because of a leak, and to be unable to do anything about it until the weekend, is an indicator of a lack of life/work balance.

Linda felt unable to delegate her problems upwards. She thought it was impossible to delegate them down as the client was questioning every single detail of every single decision, so she believed that she needed to manage everything personally. In the end she came off the account for health reasons, taking a three-month sabbatical in a Himalayan retreat to recover. Even now she finds it difficult to dwell on what happened. If you have to give that much, you're giving too much and you will never get recompensed. Sometimes you need to know when to give in and accept that you are not the person to fix the problem.

Linda asks herself now why she did not trust her intuition more and lift herself out of what became a situation that rapidly demanded more from her than she had to give. This is a good question. Once everything became personal, Linda lost her perspective and her sense of trust in her own intuition. We find that people tend to either overestimate or underestimate their intuition. It can become a magical gut feeling that is never wrong, or it becomes a feeling that contradicts the rule book and so must be ignored. Intuition cannot give you the answer to everything. It is not a quasi-mystical voice from the ether either. Of course, it can also be totally wrong, when you're not 100 per cent yourself. The point is that Linda's personal involvement and desire to triumph meant that she couldn't give herself or her boss the best advice in the situation. Sometimes in a time of trouble you have to recognise that you've lost perspective.

TROUBLE STRATEGY 7

The burnout

On the way up

If you cannot see the wood for the trees, if a situation at work is too personal, don't just go to your line manager. They will probably be too involved as well. Step outside your normal circles and find your intuitive response. Don't drown in any work crisis – it isn't worth it, and you won't benefit. Walk away from a no-win situation sooner rather than later, while you can extract yourself with your dignity and health intact. Take a deep breath, go on a proper holiday before you need to and work out how you're going to get yourself out of the pattern of behaviour before it crushes you. If any of this is familiar to you, book a holiday right now for next week.

From the top

Linda's boss should have spotted this. He should have whisked her off the account as soon as he noticed her demeanour and given her an account she could start with a fresh approach (after a week's leave). Instead, he kept offering her support (which she wasn't capable of accepting) and colluded in her demise. He didn't want to undermine her, which is admirable, but his interventions were too little and too late. Managers must analyse where the problems come from, both as an individual and a manager. And in as neutral a way as possible. There were some gender preconceptions going on here in both Linda's reactions and those of her boss. Surely Linda – the best woman they had in the business – would be able to manage this woman client? Be aware of your own – or your colleague's – pinch point and manage it.

Trouble in summary

Let us face up to the fact that we can all get ourselves into Trouble, and when we do, retribution or Nemesis can strike any of us. Yet it rarely visits those who can look at themselves with a clear perspective and acknowledge their strengths and their weaknesses equally and accurately. 'Know yourself' as the Oracle at Delphi said (to stick with our Greek theme). If you can work out objectively what you're good at and understand what you're less good at, then you have a strong foundation on which to build your career.

We hope that the tactics in this chapter will help you avoid Trouble as the consequences can be painful. Nemesis is never a reason to quit your career, though sometimes it can be a catalyst to changing your role, team or even company. But if you do find yourself in self-inflicted Trouble, then remember that if you learn from it, it can be the most valuable bit of training you will ever receive.

Trouble: The strategies in brief

On the way up

1. If you get yourself into trouble, stick to your principles and keep going to get yourself out of it. Don't put the brakes on, accelerate.

2. If you don't like the tone of the banter around you, do something about it. It's a good idea to give as good as you get.

3. If you do do something you wish could stay private, and it doesn't, either brazen it out or deny. The best tactic is: JDDI (Just Don't Do It).

4. If you need mentoring, find a mentor who has nothing to do with your past or, in fact, your present.

5. Never deviate from your true self.

6. If you can't win the fight, it may be better to give way for now.

7. Don't drown in any work crisis – it isn't worth it. Walk away from a no-win situation sooner rather than later, while you can extract yourself with dignity.

From the top

1. Any boss needs to be flexible in how they deal with their team. If you aren't, don't expect everyone to like it or to put up with it.

2. A good manager ensures that everyone in the team feels welcome. If you have an exclusively barrack-room culture, you won't attract a range of great people.

3. As the boss, stand by your talented people whatever they get up to, but give them this chapter to read.

4. One size doesn't fit all, and the investment in people will pay back in spades. Make sure people know that you're there to get the best from them and then DO IT.

5. As a company, regularly work on whether your company has an 'inclusive' culture. That you create the environment for talent to shine, rather than employ the same old types and then expect a different outcome.

6. As team leader, step in, restore confidence, move on.

7. As team leader, you need to diagnose what's going on and deal with it.

ONE VOICE: RACHEL

Rachel is about to return to work from her second maternity leave. Is it time to reconsider her route to the top?

'I'm due to go back to work in a few months, after my third baby is a year old, but I think I'm probably going to go back a little earlier to ease myself in. Have a couple of months of starting three days and working back up to four. There are lot of emotions at the moment really. I'm thinking about what's really right for everybody in my family at the moment. Not just about what I want from work and what I want from my career. I'm thinking what's right for my sons, daughter and our family life.

If I'm honest, I feel like I need a couple of months to get myself back into work and get my head together before I go all guns blazing into the next stage of my career. For me, I was lucky to have children at a point where I chose and really wanted to have children. They came quite quickly. But it was also a point in my career when I was just about to take the next step up. So for the last two to three years I've been content in not having to think about that, but I don't think I'll have any more children now. So suddenly I feel a bit under pressure. I suddenly have to think, hang on, it's not just about what happens next with babies and maternity leaves, it's really for me to choose now. What kind of life do I want? What do I want next? I'm really happy with my current employer, and I'm very lucky to have a supportive employer and environment at work, which not many women have. I've got the flexibility to do a challenging job and work part-time if I want to. I'm very lucky, but I feel a little bit stuck because it's the first time for ages that I've had that freedom really.

'It's quite a strange feeling as I've spent ages bound by babies! I've realised that I wouldn't want to be a stay-at-home mum. I feel guilty about that sometimes. I'm surrounded by a lot of women, who were working as bankers and lawyers before they had babies, who didn't have the flexibility in returning to work that I have. They're in jobs where they have to work five days a week. This makes me feel very lucky.

'But it also makes me think: I could just work three days a week if I wanted to, but I'm not sure that I want to. And a weird guilt comes with that because I think people say, "Oh, you can do three days then", but if I want to do well in my job and career, I don't think I could do that in a three-day week. And I'm feeling anxious about my twins starting pre-school this autumn. That's a new thing for me – I've always had babies who can't do much, and suddenly I have these little people who are relying on me. So that's something else I'm thinking about. What about when they start school and need help with homework? Can women have it all? It's not a black-and white-thing, it's about do women want it all?

'I don't see how a woman can physically be there and do everything. I personally feel like our generation do have choices, maybe some professions more so than others. If you want to be there for homework etc., I can't see how you can do the five-day-week, high-level jobs. From what I can see, women are either choosing to do that or not. So it's a really tough time going back to work. There are a million and one questions … I feel quite overwhelmed in truth. Lots of new thoughts have come into my mind about work and my career – things I hadn't thought of before. It's not just about "Can I pick up the kids on time. What's the childcare situation?" It's also about our family life. I'm thinking more about what my husband is doing and what the family needs.

'Whether or not you have the most supportive husband in the world, there are different demands. I don't think men get the same flexibility, which then impacts on me. It's all very well saying three-day week, four-day week, flexible hours for me when my husband doesn't have that option. So that already puts working mums in certain positions that we wouldn't choose. At some point in the next few months I need to think about what I want to do. I haven't had that headspace to do that yet. I feel so lucky to have the job I have, so that supersedes everything. So it could easily take me a good six to twelve months to come to terms with all of that before I think about what I want.

Back to equality in the workplace – I feel very removed from statistics and theory. My mum is very tuned in to feminism. She's of a generation that needed to fight. She's a real fighter and campaigner about these issues. But I haven't had to have that struggle. But I don't think it's any easier for us as women, despite some of the equality issues being addressed openly. We're still a very anxious group of mums coming back to work. We're still hormonal and emotional from giving birth. You still have this struggle that men don't have.

'I know some men, some dads, walk out of the door and don't think about what the kids are doing and what they're eating. Mums have to. I think: hang on a minute, I'm doing all this home stuff and working, and that's with the best husband in the world. What about women who don't have a supportive home life? You don't share the load equally when you go back to work because men aren't programmed to think like that. I've got a great nanny, so I am lucky, but it's still two full-time jobs. A lot of women I know don't have nannies. Last time I found it stressful, having to leave at five, all day I was worrying about having to leave work at a certain time. That's another thing I found stressful last time, having to dash around and leave early, whatever the job required of me.

'I am still ambitious, although maybe not so much in terms of moving up the ladder. But I don't just coast, and I still have that fire. But I'm worse at asking for things, whereas before I'd be very demanding. I have more guilt. I went into work today and I was sort of saying, "Thanks for having me back" – I was apologetic. I'm more on the back foot. Day to day I'm just as ambitious, but I'm more grateful now when I get given a break or a step up – but why do I feel like that? I shouldn't, as I'm due that. My ambition is still there, but I'm a bit more chilled out about having it all now. I met a really interesting woman at a woman's network. She was probably late fifties, and she had a high-powered job, but her career had taken a back seat for the last ten years and she was saying, don't let that put you off. Don't think that is the end of your career. My mum is a role model for me. Her career took off in her forties, she was in her peak in her fifties and she will probably do that well into her seventies. Mum can't imagine not working then. So this woman's message was: don't waste those precious years worrying about promotion. Stand still a bit. Have a job you like and enjoy. Why do we have to do it all now? So I think actually, for the next few years (it's not for ever, is it?) I should give myself a break and just see how it goes. I've had friends who have given up their jobs. And they don't end up going back to work. For me it's so important to stay in it. Maybe I will do three days a week, but you've got to stay in it. I don't know if that's right, though. To be fair, if men gave up their jobs for five years, they might lose their confidence too.

'It's very important to me to be a role model to my kids. I love being with the kids. But it is important to me to work. And that's not a judgement on other women. Most working women I know do after hours. Men supporting more is my bugbear. I don't think it's fair on women. We need to be able to rely on our other halves or ask them for help. I know when I was doing nursery pick-ups, there were a few dads there. But it seemed like a big deal or a big drama around it when they were.

'I do find some of the advice around women needing to be more pushy difficult – I just don't really agree with it. A lot of the theory, and the rules about getting on as a woman at work, I actually find a bit stressful. Sometimes you just want to be – not constantly thinking should I be doing this, should I be doing that. Sometimes that's more stressful than the work itself.'

CHAPTER 5

RESILIENCE

Men take things in their stride that
can seem to throw women off course

....

I s the glass half empty or half full? Researchers have shown that your answer may indicate how optimistic or pessimistic you are by nature and that this may link to your resilience. (Though our favourite answer is the engineer's joke 'the glass is too big'!) If your outlook is negative, then your brain could be hardwired differently from people who are more optimistic. Dr Jason Moser, one of the authors of the Michigan State University study on this topic, says that the inability to stay positive when times get tough might be hardwired into some people's brains: 'This suggests they have a really hard time putting a positive spin on difficult situations and actually make their negative emotions worse even when they are asked to think positively.'

Women are twice as likely as men to suffer from anxiety, according to this 2014 research. It's no good just telling anyone to stop worrying. You can, however, practise techniques of resilience, and experience will improve your perspective. Moser concludes: 'You can't just tell (people) to think positively or to not worry – that's probably not going to help them. So you need to take another tack and perhaps ask them to think about the problem in a different way, to use different strategies.'

You do have to be resilient, you have to have perspective, you have to bounce back. When you fall down, pick yourself up, start again. How do you gain the strength to do this – particularly after a nasty fall from a great height?

The VIA Institute (a not-for-profit organisation) has developed a peer-reviewed Character Strength Survey, which has twenty-four classifications intended to drive resilience under six main headers: wisdom and knowledge; courage and emotional strength; humanity or interpersonal skills; justice; temperance (strengths that protect; for example, forgiveness and humility); and transcendence (humour, forgiveness and spirituality).

Throughout this book you'll find strategies and tactics to develop a playbook to build strength for climbing the career ladder, but since in one specific area a lack of resilience might be costing you significant amounts of money, let's get to this strategy here.

Authors Linda Babcock and Sara Laschever explain, in their book *Why Women Don't Ask*, the root causes of the reality uncovered by their research that men are four times more likely to ask for higher pay than women with the same qualifications. They date it back to those childhood games we mention in Chapter 1. They say that girls are likely to play in small groups and seek to increase intimacy and prefer consensus. In contrast, boys play in larger groups, and their play is rougher. They order each other around, and there's more conflict, competition and struggle for dominance. In the process they learn that they can be aggressive without really hurting each other. They learn that competition is fun, that the opposing side can still be friends and that asserting themselves can mean a win. Women have less opportunity to practise this while growing up, and lack the social reinforcement to do so. So, in the workplace, they're less good at it to begin with. In addition, in the UK at least, girls are less likely to play or even watch team sports once they become teenagers, or as young adults. This can influence our ambition and our resilience, and, as we've seen in Chapter 1, there is a well-researched corollary between playing sports growing up and the base of current women leaders. This does not mean that you aren't heading for the top if you skipped games at school, but it does mean that you may need to work on your resilience specifically, and this chapter will explain how to do this.

Learning that a disappointment in negotiation can be a springboard, and that conflict in the office is not personal, is essential to shape your career to the desired outcome. Since Babcock and Laschever's book claims that by neglecting to negotiate the starting salary for her first job a woman may sacrifice over a quarter of a million pounds in earnings by the end of her career, let's start with a case study about Dani's resilience in asking for a pay rise.

CASE STUDY 1

Don't ask, don't get

Asking for a pay rise can feel terrifying, and as if it is just not within your personality, for a lot of women. Even for people who are used to negotiating on behalf of their clients, it can feel alien to negotiate for themselves. If you prepare sufficiently, however, it can prove so profitable that you will begin to take it in your stride.

Dani remembers very well the first time she was driven to demand a pay rise. 'I was doing well at my new job,' she recalls, 'I was put on the board of the company only six months after joining, and I was really thrilled. Then I made a discovery that caused me sleepless nights for a week.'

Dani found out that of the three people who had been promoted at the same time, she was the only one who had not received a pay rise. She was also the only woman. She was outraged. 'I went and cornered the CEO. I was very, very upset. I said that I could only conclude that it was a gender issue. He totally denied it. Then two days later he called me back into his office and gave me a huge pay rise.'

Dani had been so outraged that she felt that it was within her rights to demand a raise. Even when she had received the rise, though, she was still upset, and it took her a while, several months in fact, to settle back into a good working relationship with her CEO.

Every business will be trying to get the most out of its workforce and to control its salary bill.

Dani's CEO thought that the business could simply promote Dani and that she'd be so pleased that they could delay her pay review. He was wrong. Was it a crime that he tried? Was it an outrage that she had to ask for what she wanted?

Work is not your family, your friendship circle or school. While a good work culture should be fair and should bring out the best in everyone, not all work cultures are equal in this respect. Dani's boss didn't know her that well, as she had only been working for him for six months. He saw her as diligent and efficient. He had no idea what she would or would not put up with as far as pay was concerned. He tried something he thought that he could get away with. She explained that he was wrong, she set him straight. As far as he was concerned, he learned something about her and then moved on. In her head she had been exploited and she was very upset. Now, with the benefit of hindsight and years' more experience, she can see that she was subject to what some call the 'Tiara Syndrome', a term coined by Dr Deborah Kolb and Carol

Frohlinger from Negotiating Women, a US firm that coaches women in leadership skills, because women 'sit there thinking the work I'm doing is so great someone will come along and they'll put a tiara on my head [while] at the next desk, is going to be a young man who has perhaps done one terrific thing and has no embarrassment about jumping on his desk … and saying to the CEO: "look at me, look at me, aren't I fabulous?"' Dani knew she was valued, and she expected to be rewarded as a result without having to ask for that reward – in financial terms, as well as by being given a new title.

Dani's boss thought he'd see if he could get away with the title with no pay rise. When he didn't, he shrugged, gave her the money and was ready to move on. She was stuck with a sense of outrage for ages. In the long run this might have been valuable to her career development anyway. As we will go on to see in a subsequent chapter, anger is a great motivator. Here are three steps to asking for a pay rise, and none of them need deeply upset you once you wrap your head around the fact that no one pays anyone more than they think that they have to. That's just how business works.

Three steps to asking for a pay rise

Step 1 The prep

This is not only about making sure that your work is in order. It is also, and most crucially, about ensuring that you have a good close working relationship with the person who is deciding your pay rise. Make sure that you are visible to them (see Chapter 3). Make sure that they think that you value them. Get them on your side. Do not despair if you don't currently have that relationship – this kind of thing can be turned around. Make some timely requests for their advice (bosses love to be asked for their help – try the words 'Only you, with your experience, can help me with this'). Thank them for their input with a few judicious emails quoting things that they have said to you that you have acted on. Find a way to like them, and they will like you back.

Step 2 Propaganda

This needs to happen before you ask for the raise. Your boss needs to understand that you are an independent person who is attractive to other companies – especially your company's competition. They need to understand that you will not cling endlessly to your job and that you might move on. Many women find this idea actually quite upsetting because they have invested emotionally in the relationship with their current firm, or indeed, their boss themselves. Just because you are issuing this propaganda does not mean that you are actually leaving. This is a campaign. It is acting. Your boss needs to think that he is more dependent on you than the other way round. For instance, you might drop casually into conversation that a friend of yours was asking if you knew anyone who could join their firm. Be subtle here, however.

Step 3 The ask

Go in knowing what you are worth. If you are turned down, try not to leave empty-handed. Negotiate, for a time period, for a clear understanding of what the specific barriers are to your raise and help with overcoming them. Understand that, even if it feels personal, it probably isn't. Your boss is just responding with the company line. Look, you may get what you want immediately – in which case, well done you. But if not, then give your boss some time to come up with a compromise solution. But don't ask, not get and then give up. Fix a time there and then when you can revisit the question.

Don't ask, don't get

On the way up

It is important to ask for what you want and to negotiate in the least personal way possible. Your role is to maximise the amount you are paid for your services. Your boss's role is to control the cost of the talent he employs. Make sure that you prepare the ground well in advance.

From the top

You want to grow your talent. This means treating them as if they are adults, not dismissing their negotiations out of hand. Don't exploit your talent. But if you have to say no to them, then don't intimidate and do get back to your talent with an alternative offer.

CASE STUDY 2

When to walk away

There is no clear answer to this dilemma. Some people are happy to have the groove of a long-term, known position and use their knowledge of the organisation to develop skills and talents that might not be available to a newer, less familiar personality. Your company might see you expanding your horizons as a way to keep you motivated as well as creating a diverse 'bench' of people that makes it more attractive to clients.

Other people move at certain fixed periods – say, three years – as they get bored with the organisation and what it offers them. We've all known the chaps who use their moves (or threatened moves) as a way of expanding their role or pay packet. Beware though – after a while, too regular moves can make your CV look patchy.

That sense of when to walk away has many sources. Most are from within, but occasionally they can be an external push that makes you appraise whether it's time to go.

Kara is a talented and hard-working woman who has huge personal charm and drive. She left school at eighteen, tired of the academic focus and just wanting to get on with her career. Eventually she found herself as a PA in an organisation where the management was universally educated to degree level (sometimes to an even higher level) and also mostly male. Over time Kara demonstrated that she was a huge asset to the whole company: organised, creative and able to get anyone 'on side'. People loved being around her, and her role became increasingly outward-focused. Moving from the role of a PA to business development helped her blossom: internally, she was able to get teams of people to work together cohesively, and, externally, her charisma and work ethic were highly valued.

She was very successful and eventually promoted to the most senior role in business development. She threw herself into it, and her company benefited from it. She was widely known as someone who delivered, and she worked incredibly hard to maximise this opportunity – she was the driving force of revenue into the company and was helping to create its future. Accepted and valued, she had found her niche and loved her role.

One small incident, however, changed all that.

Working on a massive new project proposal, Kara was the driver of the whole enterprise. She worked continually for months, becoming so tired that she fell asleep in the cabs that took her home in the early hours of the morning and getting in as dawn broke to ensure that she kept on top of the other elements of her role. As the big day of the proposal presentation approached, everyone involved was working towards delivering a proposal that would wow the client. Kara was the glue holding it together. The day before the meeting the whole team and the senior management were due to have a rehearsal at 2.30 p.m. to make sure that there were no glitches.

As she put the final touches to the room, a male colleague walked by. 'Wow, what a lot of work this has been,' he said. Kara agreed, thinking of her broken nights and unanswered emails. She had fallen asleep when she'd gone to see her parents on the one afternoon off she'd taken at the weekend. (Her mum, faced with the idea that Kara was working a six-day week and had fallen asleep on the sofa in their sitting room despite the beautiful sunny weather, consoled her by saying, 'Well, at least you won't run the risk of sunburn.')

'So, as I'm the first to talk, you could pop out and get me a sandwich, couldn't you? Tuna would be great and maybe a Coke?' her male colleague now requested.

Kara looked at him and realised that, to a whole swathe of her peers, she would always be a PA who got lucky.

She left within three months. She is now at a very senior level in a multinational company.

RESILIENCE STRATEGY 2

When to walk away

On the way up

Draw the line. Yes, throw yourself at your career, but make sure that you have a very clear line and that no one crosses it.

From the top

If you exploit your talent, it will either burn out or leave. No one is suggesting that your job is to run an organisation of prima donnas, but you need to make sure that the open-top bus is available for people when they've put the effort it. Care for your people, don't allow the signals from the top to be dis- extracurricular effort, and it will pay off.

The secret rules of work

Phillip is a senior partner at a law firm in London. He suggests caution when we ask him about gender equality: 'Be careful of your angle, some things take forever to change, and voicing your sense of inequality can make things worse.

'Yes, there are more senior men in my sector than women. Partly because we mirror and reflect the culture of our clients; often because we are basically complying with a set of unwritten rules that are baked into the world.'

Phillip is referring to 'Cryptonomics', the kind that operate in the workplace. Management consultant Peter Scott-Morgan has described systems of hidden rules that any workplace operates by but that no one will tell you about. All workplaces have these rules. Unless you gain an understanding of them, every setback can feel personal. If you find out what the rules of the game are, then you can choose to play by them, or to break them, or to walk away. Phillip may be voicing the concerns of those who wish to preserve the status quo, and you might choose to disagree with him. Either way, understand the rules before you break them; don't knock them over accidentally and pay the price.

Jasmine has three children, aged nine, six and three. Her husband is a TV cameraman. This means that his hours tend to be sporadic. He can be home for long stretches during the day. He can fly to the other side of the world for weeks at a time with very little notice. Jasmine can't count on him for childcare certainty. Her job is regular: she's an Executive Assistant to a CEO. Her boss is demanding, but not unfair. He expects her life to be as regular now as it ever used to be.

Jasmine is aware that this is ridiculous. To begin with, when her children were very young (at least now they're all at school or pre-school), she felt as though she was constantly apologising for having to leave early to cater for their needs. Now, she just fibs. 'I would say to any mother, if you need to stay home because one of your children is sick, don't tell the truth. Say that you feel ill. No one will question you, you're not going to do this every week. If you say that you're staying at home because of a child having a temperature, everyone will disapprove of you. Even if it means that essentially, because you are healthy, you could work from home. The men with stay-at-home wives will disapprove of you and think that you're unreliable. People without children will think that your priorities are wrong, they will not understand. Fib – it's easier, you'll get more sympathy, and you won't lose respect.'

Jasmine, it is worth saying, has never fibbed much about anything else in her life. But her career was slipping into a downward spiral, as she came across one of the unwritten rules of her office: it is not OK to stay at home if your child has a temperature. We're not referring to serious illness here – that's completely different. We're talking about the minor bugs that all kids get, and all mums worry about. Yet they worry a lot, and Jasmine rationalises that she would be worried sick if she didn't stay at home anyway.

Before she had children, Jasmine had no idea about this unwritten, and yet very strong, secret and unofficial rule. Before she understood this rule, Jasmine felt guilty all the time. Now she doesn't. She takes it in her stride. She's pragmatic. Her work hasn't suffered. Nor, actually, has her moral compass. Where before she had felt diminished, now she feels triumphant.

Such rules don't just affect mums. There are all kinds of rules in business. The official rules about behaviour and how things should work may well be written down in a handbook. But as business coach Bonnie Marcus explains, the unwritten rule is probably the opposite and is nearly always more powerful. She says: 'There may be formal rules for how the company operates, but not everyone follows them. In fact, the more attention you pay to the workplace dynamics, the more you will realise that there are many unwritten rules that no one tells you about. As a result, you are forced to discover them through trial and error, and in the process you can find yourself in a sensitive situation. It's up to you to figure out what all the rules are at your company to be successful.'

The written rule will say, for instance, that the company's organogram indicates who has the power to tell people what to do. In reality, this is rarely how things work. If you have been promoted, don't expect your title to confer authority or respect. It rarely does, and you have to earn it. In addition, decisions are rarely made by one person. Many people influence decisions, and sometimes politics trumps titles. Don't assume that someone's position means that this person has power. Look carefully to see who makes the decisions and who influences those decisions. These people need to be on your radar screen if you want to get ahead. You might think that you can announce a change or what you want to do. When it doesn't happen as you've planned, because, although everyone agreed, there has been no real compliance, you might feel disappointed and frustrated. Instead, you need to think about how you announced your decision. Should you have consulted some of your team privately first to make sure that they would support you? Is someone in the team agreeing to what you said in public, but in private doing the opposite? If they are undermining you subtly, then it is unlikely to be possible to sack them or even to discipline them. Especially if they're popular. You've come up against an unwritten rule. Once you understand it, you can stop wasting your time being angry or frustrated. You can instead work out how to deal with it.

Unwritten rules can be easy to bend to your own advantage. Some commentators think that we should ignore them because they're not fair or right. One executive director of an organisation promoting opportunities for women calls them 'ridiculous, and just perpetuating illusions'. That may well be true. We think that, if you can easily use them to promote your image in the office and to help you to overcome the disadvantages that often still result from society's framing of gender, then of course you should do so. In other words, it can't hurt to: sit near the CEO in a meeting; send an email late at night or early in the morning to show how seriously you take the job; walk fast round the building and never stroll; never pour the tea and coffee if you are the only woman in the meeting.

None of this is a substitute for doing your job well, but where men seem to instinctively look out for the unwritten rules and exploit them, women insist on fairness. Until you're the boss, there's no point. (And there may be no point even then – those unwritten rules exist and have power.) Look for the secret rules and work them to your advantage.

The secret rules of work

On the way up

Understand that there are two kinds of rules in every organisation: the written rules and the secret, unwritten rules. Work them out, exploit them. This can take time, but if you look for them, then at least you will understand them more easily. The reason that some new brooms who are brought in to change or revitalise companies fail is because they tackle the written rules only. Even if they have changed reward programmes and management structures, there is such a strong set of secret rules and behaviours that the effort is in vain. Once you know the secret rules, feel free either to break them as Jasmine did, or to exploit them for your benefit. Don't get defeated by them.

From the top

The fewer secret rules in your organisation, the healthier it will be. However, don't kid yourself that they don't exist because you don't want them to. Be actively aware and don't reinforce them.

The numbers game

Briony is a director at a global media company. She spares some time with us for breakfast and to share her experiences of work, of family life (she has a young family) and of ensuring a balance between the two.

'It is tough,' she admits. 'Women want everything to be perfect, at home and at work. Eventually you have to accept that it can't be. But you do have to assert yourself at home, as well as at work. Women who have run teams with hundreds of people don't always have the wherewithal to say no to their partners.'

She points to one of the contrasts between men and women: the numbers game. 'Blokes are used to playing a numbers game in dating. Ask enough times and it will work. Men grow up knowing that there will be a next time. Women give everything a huge dramatic edge.'

She seems to be on to something here. Women don't always ask for what they want in case they get turned down. Men seem instinctively to understand that, if they don't ask, then they definitely won't get what they want, but also, and perhaps more crucially, that the very act of asking makes a positive answer more likely in the long run.

Lettie wants a promotion. She has been in her role for eighteen months and knows that she is doing well. She is hungry for the next step. The unwritten rule of her company, which she has come to understand, is that no one gets promoted until a spot in senior management is freed up by someone leaving. This did not appear to be on the cards in the near future. Should she wait, like a good girl, and see what happens? Or should she break with the status quo and go and ask for what she wants?

Lettie decides to go for it. She sets up a meeting with her boss and sets out her reasons for being promoted. She reviews her achievements. She gives testimonies that she has solicited from her clients. Her boss says, in summary, that things are looking pretty bleak for her division this year and that promotions are not on the cards. Now what? Lettie has a lot of emotion riding on this encounter. Should she go back to her desk and lick her wounds? Absolutely not. Instead, she says, 'I will spend some time thinking of ways that we can improve things. I'm coming back to see you in a week with a set of ideas that will improve efficiencies and help us with a step change.'

Lettie not only spends time preparing for this meeting – she also looks ahead. She mentions to her boss's boss that she is having this meeting, and will share the ideas with him too. She fixes the next meeting for a week away and is determined that, even if she comes out of it with nothing, she will fix another meeting in six weeks to have another conversation. Lettie's resilience is impressive. It does pay off. The next time an opening for promotion comes up in another department, her boss puts her forward for it. Normally he would have just ignored an opportunity in another team. He has got the message loud and clear from Lettie. She's not going away. She's going to continue to bounce into his office with ideas, with suggestions and with requests.

When the new role is suggested to Lettie, she's a bit taken aback. She wanted a promotion in her current division. Suddenly there are all those doubts that we have all experienced. Is she up to a bigger job in another part of the company? Lettie now has to overcome another numbers game bias that seems especially female. It is well documented that men will apply for jobs if they can do about half of what seems to be required on the job spec. Women need to feel that they can manage all of it.

Remember that Hewlett-Packard study (in Chapter 1) that found that men apply for a job when they consider themselves 60 per cent qualified for it, while women won't raise their hands until they feel 100 per cent qualified?

Writer Joanne Lipman feels strongly that men need to recognise this as well as women. She writes: 'Men are often clueless about the myriad ways in which they misread women in the workplace every day. Not intentionally. But wow.

They misunderstand us, they unwittingly belittle us, they do something that they think is nice that instead just makes us mad. And those are the good ones.'

In Lettie's case, when the promotion is offered, she does have her doubts because it is not exactly what she has asked for. Does she have the experience necessary? She is really not so sure now. Perhaps her boss is particularly keen to get her promotion sorted out because there is a steely determination about Lettie's encounters with him that make it very clear that Lettie will not shut up and sit down or go away. So when Lettie voices her doubts about being qualified for the promotion in another division, her boss makes it clear that she should not worry – he will support her (he now thinks of her as an ally) and she will have a good team to manage.

Are too many women ruling themselves out for big roles? Does the risk seem too high to jump to a senior position?

Lipman would perhaps suggest that we need the men occupying these roles currently to understand that women need pushing or coaxing into them.

We believe women need to be a bit more laid back about the numbers game. Ask enough times and you will get what you want. If you feel half qualified, you're probably twice as qualified as anyone else applying for the role.

RESILIENCE STRATEGY 4

The numbers game

On the way up

Don't get put off. Keep asking for what you want. If you don't get it, ask again. And take a bit of a chance on whether you're qualified for a new role. Chances are you will find it easier than you think.

From the top

Understand that men and women have different perceptions of the numbers game and act accordingly. Think about how you say no to your female talent.

CASE STUDY 5

The playbook

People aren't born resilient. It isn't a gift or talent. You can create circumstances that help you to build resilience, and it doesn't require a massive effort. You need a set of techniques, a playbook, that you can fall back on in times of difficulty or stress.

Resilience is a process. By learning to accept the situation as it is and taking a long-term view, you're putting distance between what has happened and your personal reaction to the situation. This helps to prevent it from being all about you. Once you start moving on from your first response to a setback being 'Oh no, it's a disaster', you're moving in the right direction. So many people exacerbate tricky situations by assuming that it is all going to end very, very badly.

If there is a typo in your document and it's too late to change it before the meeting starts, your client is very unlikely to fire your company as a result.

Be realistic. You aren't going to learn to speak and write Mandarin in a year to get that big job in Shanghai, particularly if you need to work full-time in the interim. That may sound completely obvious, but it was said by a colleague we know. He advised the China-focused person that maybe it would be better to have timely and realistic goals to get them to Shanghai rather than aiming for the moon, missing it and then saying that you always fail. You fail when you either don't appreciate what can get you to your goal and whether or not it's achievable OR if you can achieve it but you don't put the effort in. There is no point thinking that you'll never get promoted in your current company if you don't actually step up and apply for jobs. You aren't a neglected genius: you're just moaning in the corner if you fail to assess what's needed.

By being positive about your skills and abilities you have, you are building your sense of self. By having a developed sense of who you are and what you can do (rather than thinking about what you can't do), you are self-renewing. Most organisations are a matrix of talents, and you play your part in that. They probably have someone who can do what you can't, so don't worry about it.

Developed communication and problem-solving skills add to your resilience base. Rarely are big problems solved by one person, and being able to articulate what the issue is and your perspective on it brings clarity. Know what the issue is, have a plan to address it and tell everyone what it is.

Problems bring a lot of things in their wake. One person we spoke to remembered being at a company where their biggest client announced that they were moving their business elsewhere. Gathering the senior team together, the CEO told them what had happened, that there was no chance of winning them back and that it would be common knowledge later that day. One person started shouting, another one was shaking, nearly on the verge of tears. Another person was saying, 'Well, we're all going to lose our jobs, aren't we? Oh no, what will I do?' The only calm person was the CEO.

Later on, he confided to our contact that he was calm because he knew that the company could get over this loss, that the owners had assured him that job losses would be limited to natural wastage and that he had a plan. But he didn't get a chance to articulate that because people had just let their emotions out. Although it was a shock, none of his team had asked what the plan was. He joked that maybe they thought he didn't have a clue what to do.

To maintain your resilience it is important to have a perspective on your work. Here are three quick resilience tips to start your personal playbook with.

An eighteen-hour day followed by fitful sleep isn't a recipe for success in the long term. All people with strong resilience skills have an outlet: baking, yoga, running. You need something that is just for you.

Family and friends provide a support network that values you for being you, not the targets you just smashed. They are your team, and they can offer you a perspective that is completely different to the world of work.

Keep developing your skills. Enhance ones you already have, or find some new ones that interest you.

The playbook

On the way up

You need to develop a playbook of tactics to deploy when times are tough and you can't think. This could be going for a walk round the block instead of collapsing. It could be learning new techniques or skills every year.

From the top

Everyone needs a playbook, and you've probably already got one as the leader of your team. Share it. Help your talent develop resilience too.

Don't take it personally

There is a scene in the ultimate Hollywood view of females and fashion *The Devil Wears Prada* that never fails to make us smile. The devil of the title, Miranda Priestly, is hosting a massive party and her assistants are tasked with memorising the names and jobs of the entire guest list: three huge books that clearly contain many, many names. The purpose of this is to ensure that Miranda appears to recall every one of the invitees. This party is one of the events of the season and everyone who is anyone HAS to be there.

It just goes to prove that sometimes Hollywood gets it right. Miranda just wants to look as if she knows everyone and, in turn, the guests want to be acknowledged by her. It's a situation of mutual dependency. Aiming to be memorable is utterly pointless. Everyone, but everyone, is just thinking about themselves.

Dee told us that one of the key pieces of advice that she gives to people at the start of their careers is always to speak early in meetings where they have something to add. 'If you wait too long, the discussions are more involved, and in your attempt to stand out and contribute, you may just miss the moment. Saying "I was going to say that" in an aggrieved tone isn't advised.'

Similarly, what seems of enormous importance to you can have very little impact on those around you. A female colleague was once at lunch with a client and all had gone to plan; this lunch was to help them get to know each other better, and she was delighted with the outcome. Until the moment when, as she went to pull her wallet out of her bag (all the while chatting to her contact), a tampon shot out from her bag, missing his head by inches. Barely holding it together, they finished lunch and she walked back to work, mortified. Months of red-faced shame followed as she relived that moment in her head. She knew he was a nice enough man not to have turned it into an office anecdote, but she was still so ashamed. Eventually the moment came when she felt comfortable enough to talk to him about it. He was impassive as she tentatively explained what had happened. He smiled: he'd thought she was flustered because she had inadvertently thrown a pen at him. He thought it was a mini free pen from retailer Argos and that was the issue. It had never occurred to him that it was anything else.

Another contact advises that acting as the 'scribe' can be a good tactic in some meetings. 'So many people just want to come in and talk, hog the limelight and get noticed. If you're the scribe, you are taking charge, collating the information and giving the feedback. It also shows that you're a team player, not an ego on legs. We want people who are problem-solvers, who can assimilate information and deliver it back in a coherent manner. Too often people assume the limelight is the place to be. The key is in how you handle yourself within the team.'

It is so easy to assume that your progress and your career are as consuming to your boss as they are to you. That isn't the case. They want happy, stable and productive teams. They have to think about the whole of the group, not just you. So when they don't praise you for doing a good job, don't assume it isn't noticed. It's another tick in the box of your good work.

Be as objective about yourself as you can when you think about your career. We've talked in other parts of this book about the importance of you and your 'brand'.

Don't take it personally

On the way up

Basically, do not take anything personally. If you feel slighted or overlooked take a breath. Put yourself in the other person's shoes – what's going on from their perspective? How would it look if you were a bystander? Would you even pick up on the thing that has caused you stress? However embarrassing something feels like to you, it may have completely passed the bystanders by. If reacting to a situation with drama gets you boxed in as childish or demanding, it will do your career no good at all. Decide where the line is – earlier on we saw that it will do you no good to be a doormat, but don't react to everything as if it is about you. It probably isn't.

From the top

Balancing the needs of the whole team is essential. However, a well-timed bit of private and personal praise can work wonders in motivating a team member. One CEO we spoke to says that he thinks that there is nothing more powerful than breaking the rules for someone as an exception. The rule you break can be tiny ('Take the rest of the day off, take your team to the park for ice creams'), but the impact may be huge.

Resilience in summary

Dean Becker, the president and CEO of Adaptiv Learning Systems, says: 'More than education, more than experience, more than training, a person's level of resilience will determine who succeeds and who fails. That's true in the hospital ward, it's true in the Olympics, and it's true in the boardroom.'

Resilience is all about perspective and bouncing back. It

can feel like your world has ended after a bad day at work. It hasn't. There are a number of techniques described in this chapter to develop resilience, but the most fundamental one is not to give up. Take a moment, have a break; but, however tough it feels, keep going.

Resilience: The strategies in brief

On the way up

1. Plan your requests. Make your arguments for the benefit of the business, not just your personal benefit.

2. Know when to stop putting up with things. Draw a line, and stick to it. Always.

3. Make sure that you're playing by the unwritten rules of the business not just the stated ones. If you think that there aren't any, then think again. You just don't know what they are.

4. Play the numbers game. If you hear a 'no' the first time you ask for something, don't see that as the end. Keep asking.

5. Have a playbook of tactics to use in difficult times. If you have a resource to fall back on, you will feel braver and are less likely to react inappropriately.

6. Fight always to have perspective.

From the top

1. Make sure that you treat your talent as adults; if you have to say no, have a counter-offer.

2. Don't lose people because you have boxed them into a stereotype.

3. Make sure you are aware of the secret rules of your own organisation, and of who is playing games with them.

4. You should understand that the women in your team may not understand the numbers game as intuitively as the men.

5. Everyone needs a playbook.

6. Make sure that you balance the broad needs of the team with the needs everyone has from time to time for some personal praise or a private pat on the back.

ONE VOICE: MEGAN

Megan has been working at an advertising agency for just three years. It is her first job after university. She's surprised, very surprised, at the difference between how men and women her age are treated, at how they behave and how assertive they are at work. When we speak to her, she is considering how much of this she can change in order to progress where she is now, or whether she should consider looking to progress her career in a completely different way.

'I am three years into a graduate job working at a creative agency, having joined on quite a prestigious grad scheme which had all the usual difficulties and stresses in applying. I do like it, I've definitely had some big highs and big lows.

'I think the first thing I noticed when I joined was that there were a lot of women, but a lot of women of my age who were very much making the tea and sort of joining in in an enthusiastic bubbly: "it's nice to have them around" way. I think moving up to the stage where you're the person in the meeting who makes the calls and tells people in that meeting what they need to do, it's a whole different ball game. One which definitely women do, but I think when guys join the industry they're seen as a bit grumpy and up themselves. And despite people thinking that about them, guys then feel a bit more confident in their ability to be the bossy ones. There's a weird thing with girls who go from leading the charge at college to realising that at work everyone wants to have you around because you bring the mood up and ensure the meeting goes without any blips. But learning how to get on brilliantly with everyone is not the skill required for the next stage.

'I had to be the bad guy in one meeting (which you've totally got to do sometimes), and actually the minute you do it – and I now very happily do it – it's not unpleasant. In a creative agency, for example, you often get client feedback on some work and you have to go downstairs and give it to someone, and I used to be so worried about telling them that the client didn't like something. And actually they attribute that feedback to the client, not to you, so as soon as you – I hate to say, "man up", "grow some balls" – no, as soon as you "toughen up" and realise that you can tell them straight, then the conversation is totally fine and people respect you a lot more for it. That's been interesting.

'The other thing that has struck me about the world I work in is the lack of clarity from appraisal to the next step. There's no heads up on what an appraisal will be like in advance. You go in with such a panic of "My gosh, have they found me out, are they going to tell I'm terrible?" that you don't really consider what you're going to do if they tell you "you're brilliant". So then if they tell you "you're brilliant", you reach the end of the meeting high-fiving and leave. It's only when I got home that evening that I thought, "We didn't talk about pay, we didn't talk about promotion." If you went in thinking "I'm absolutely super", then you would be prepared for the conversation. It's clever; they think if they give me compliments, then I won't ask for promotion.

'It's taken me a while to understand that this is my responsibility, not theirs; after all, it is my career. I think it's a thing you toughen up to, but I wish that I had hit the ground running, that from my very first appraisal I had been ready for that next leap.

'Me and this guy are at the same level with the same boss, and he's five years older, got a baby, but he's not particularly great at his job, or particularly good with people. However, I heard this shocking news that he was getting promoted, and everyone I spoke to said that he was really pushing for it. That was groundbreaking news for me. Because I hadn't for a second thought that I needed to push for it.

'There's been quite a few examples when I've realised that boys are better at lobbying than we are. They don't find that embarrassing, they don't feel embarrassed to sit there and say, "I expect to be promoted." The guy I work with at the moment he wants to be on the board and will happily tell anyone he wants to be on the board. Whereas I think when that time came for me, I would feel quite embarrassed about it.

'It's probably, I don't know, a gender difference. Another one would probably be that in general, because of stiff upper lip and whatever, boys are better at not getting emotional in work situations. When emotion happens it totally undermines your professionalism so … it might be OK to cry in some life situations, I don't actually think it's ever OK to cry at work. I've probably cried about two or three times, and I think it takes you down about three pegs. You've got to realise that if things upset you and things stress you out, it would be better to be angry rather than cry; it would work better for you.

'Women should be advised to go for a walk when they feel emotional. I had this situation a few weeks ago, where there is this horrible person, and he works on the global piece of business and I work on the UK piece of business, and he and I have to work together. He clearly hasn't progressed as quickly in his career as he'd like. He's quite a lot older, and from the moment we've worked together he's taken offence at the fact he's expected to work with me. He always tries to talk to my boss instead of me; my boss always has to call me back in and tell him that I am running this project. This has made me feel very uncomfortable from the start. I'm not someone who feels like I've desperately got to prove myself. And actually if someone gives me a vote of un-confidence, rather than turning round and thinking "Right, I'll show you", I definitely just think, "Screw you, leave me alone."

'So I will give it the least effort possible. I won't put any effort in if this is the way you are treating me. Which is probably totally the wrong response, because I should aim to show them how good I am. But, anyway, he decided to come over to my desk at 9.07 a.m. for a conversation about whether Global would approve a creative concept (which is an issue which is littered with politics anyway). But rather than say, "We've got a few issues and we need to talk", he stood over my desk and proceeded to get more and more irate in a very public circumstance. I found this incredibly embarrassing. And it was the embarrassment of him overreacting that actually upset me. I really didn't care about his opinion on this thing. It's something that in any other manner could be discussed. When he left, I got really upset. Everyone was support-ive. They knew that I hadn't done anything wrong. And the more you evaluate it afterwards, I really didn't have any reason to feel upset. But the way he had ranted at me had really hit a nerve.

'It was the first time this had happened, because I am just three years into my career. Now, if that were to ever happen again and someone irate came over to my desk, I would say, "Shall we just go round the corner and chat about this?" and I would instantly cut it off. But the first time things happen, you kind of think, "I'll sit through this … oh my god, I'm gonna cry."

'I was pretty hysterical, to the sort of "can't breathe", the worst type of cry. He walked off and everyone goes "sharp intake of breath". Then my lovely colleague said, "Are you OK?"

'That was the trigger. That set me off. Then I sort of went to the loo, and I was so shaken and surprised. It was consuming for the rest of the day, I felt really unwell.

'He's not going to go away, so now I'm just waiting for the next encounter.

'Even under the best circumstances I have noticed that girls of my age in the office, I think we as a generation, we have often developed an upward inflection at the end of our sentences. It all comes from American movies, and it basically means everything you say sounds like a question, whether or not it is. A colleague pointed it out to me. We went to an event and he told me, "You talk about things you know the most about in the room, but you say it as though it's a question."

'So I started noticing it more and more. If you look out for it and watch young girls in teams present stuff, they present their work, and they don't sound convinced by it. I know it must have a massive effect on how much gravitas they hold in the room. You end up not really trusting them. I have seen a few women my age present work and, rather than saying "This is it, this is the answer", they're trying to win you over with a bit too much Hollywood-type nod and smile.

'You need to use words to your advantage. So if it's a rhetorical question, it shouldn't actually sound like a question. And definitely, me telling you what I did last night shouldn't sound like I'm asking you whether it's what I did last night. And the more you look out for it, the more you notice it everywhere. And you don't recognise it as what it is, you just recognise it as "they don't know their stuff. I shouldn't follow them." I've seen this in a marvellous woman in my team; when she presents work, everyone just tears the work apart. It isn't the work; it's how she speaks. Is this every workplace, or the culture of where I work? It feels like a bear pit sometimes, and I am tired of it.

'I am desperate to make sure that I have established my career before I have babies. My worst-case scenario would be to carry on as I am now, where I like bits of work, but I hate bits of it. So I know that, if I had kids, I would be torn about carrying on working. And I want to work, to build a career. The drive to want to carry on working would be much better if I found a job that I really liked. I can't work out what my niche is. That's what I want to work out now.'

CHAPTER 6

ANGER

....

Men exploit their inner bastard;
women hide the inner bitch

Anger is an energy, and it can work in three ways. Keep it inside, and it will eat you up and sap your strength. Explode with it, whether in tears or rage, or both, and you can come across as a toddler in a temper tantrum and lose respect. Use it coldly and carefully, and it can propel you to get exactly what you want.

A Harvard Medical School study a few years ago found those who repressed frustration were three times more likely to say they had reached a glass ceiling. The survey followed 824 people over forty-four years and said that it was important to remain in control when standing your ground. If you care enough about the situation that you find yourself in to be angry, then you care enough to do something about it. Most of the time that action, if a considered one, will be much more positive for the business overall than if you simply put up and shut up. This does not mean being rude. It does not mean being mean. It may well mean being disruptive to the status quo. That might be exactly what the situation needs.

People are sometimes very worried by their own anger, or even a desire for vengeance. While we are firm believers that good Karma is essential to career progression (see next chapter), we also know that faking forgiveness is bad for you too. So use your anger positively rather than suppress your feelings. We have already come across examples in earlier chapters where someone's fury about being passed over or not being treated fairly has been the catalyst to ambition or to pushing themselves into the limelight. Not all the feelings that you have at work are pretty ones. Traditional cultural stereotypes dictate that men are allowed to get noisily angry at work, whereas women are meant to be submissive or tolerant.

Evidence from Arizona State University about jury room deliberations in fact suggests that angry women lose credibility but angry men gain it even when all of the arguments are the same. Given that you can't actually get rid of your anger at will, this can mean that you end up sulking or being passively aggressive instead. Neither is good for your career. Never let those feminine stereotypes dictate your behaviour. Staying true to yourself means acknowledging every part of your persona. As a woman, you may need to channel your anger rather than shout it out, as people in general are more forgiving of men shouting than of women. This means that when you do show you are angry it will have much more impact. But showing your anger is not always the best way, as we come on now to see.

Here are some ways to channel the energy of fury into propelling your career progression.

CASE STUDY 1

Power grip

Angela works for a big manufacturer in the finance department. She has risen to a senior position through hard work, but she feels like an outsider. She's conscious that her background is not anything like that of her colleagues. She grew up in Australia, and can't share many of their cultural references, for a start. But really it is the same old story again. She is one of two women in the department, and the predominant culture of banter and put-downs is hard to cope with. Recently they had an outside trainer who asked everyone what they did to relax at the weekend. When she said, 'Yoga', one of her more senior colleagues immediately asked, 'Naked yoga, I bet that gets you all hot and steamy?' and snickered. Frankly she is sick of it. There is fairly constant, very low-level, undermining by the chaps. It's nothing that she has felt worthy of turning into anything as serious as a formal complaint, but she is feeling stressed, not about the work, not about her key performance indicators, but by the so-called friendly banter from her colleagues.

She has decided to take no more of it and hatches a plan to change the balance of power at the next possible opportunity. It comes in the next team meeting, which she chairs. As a result of the training that the team had recently undergone, the very same colleague suggested a warm-up. 'Let's all go round the table and say what car we have and what it says about us?'

Interesting, this particular warm-up, as it allows boasting about status, of course. Angela is inspired by her latent anger. She responds, leaning forward and looking him directly in the eye: 'Absolutely, we can do that. Or we can get on with the crucial business issues at hand. I suggest that we save comparing cars until we have resolved our more serious discussion.'

End of banter, end of low-level challenge. Angela has taken the balance of power back into her own hands. She has forced a re-evaluation of her status within the business. She goes on to make sure that she is the one who makes the unpopular point in any meeting. And she insists on not being fobbed off.

For instance, she questions the cost of project managers with three senior male colleagues. They say, 'Let's take that offline, Angela' (meaning 'shut up and take it off the record'), 'are you happy with that?' She says, for the minutes, 'No actually I am not.'

Her anger has prompted her bravery, and now there is no holding her back. At the same time she goes out of her way to ensure that she is not isolated by forging closer ties with the only other woman in the team. She takes her for coffee breaks. She sweeps her off for shopping trips. She seizes the power very consciously, driven by her experiences when, for years, the power eluded her. And now she has it, she will not let it go. She begins to set her own boundaries very clearly, in terms of hours worked, travel and how she is treated.

Power grip

On the way up

Angela had had enough. While her colleagues did not cross the line in any outstanding way, not a day went by without some comment that she found mildly embarrassing. Until the day she asserted herself and took back control. She began to think of power as a concrete object in the room, a bit like a talking stick. Only one person could hold it at a time, and she was determined in the future that it would always be hers. Her body language changed at the same time as what she said. No more sidling into a room as if she wasn't sure whether she belonged. She enters rooms now as if she belongs there, and despite being just 5 feet 3 inches tall, she takes up as much space as she can. She smiles less, and when she does smile, it is a full-on beam designed to have an impact. Otherwise, she is straight-faced. No more nervous grins. Never a giggle. Harvard Business School professor Amy Cuddy delivered a brilliant talk at TED (the online conference forum for spreading ideas) about the power pose and the impact it has on women's confidence. Certain 'power poses' don't just change how others perceive you, Professor Cuddy says. They immediately change your body chemistry. These changes affect the way you do your job and interact with other people. Never sit nervously, therefore, on the edge of the chair, and don't hug yourself in a meeting. Sit up, be assertive, own the room.

From the top

It is often difficult for a woman to be assertive. They are socially groomed to believe that they are being difficult or arrogant when they stand up and out and declare their differences from the rest of the group. Women are more likely to be conditioned to be agreeable in order to be liked and they confuse being liked with being successful. You may need to encourage the women who work for you to be assertive and to say what they really think. This will be useful for your business. They are using energy to suppress fury at being undermined and need to be told to stand up for themselves. Once they begin to do so, you will find them even more effective, and if you are the one who allows their anger to turn into positive energy, you will probably have their loyalty for life.

CASE STUDY 2

Odd one out

All workplaces have their own peculiarities and quirks. Some of these are a result of the desire to create a certain culture;

others come about as a consequence of the people who work there. It's important to have an understanding of how the culture works before you decide to work somewhere, as you may find that you're right for the job but not the organisation. An interesting analogy that someone used to describe their experience of this situation is that work felt like a pair of slightly too tight shoes; you could walk about in them, but it never quite felt comfortable. And the relief of taking those shoes off was intense …

Anna was really enjoying her new role and the challenges it brought. It had been a long process to get this job, and the company was going through a lot of change. It was an exciting time, and she was relishing the opportunity. The one issue that stopped her being completely happy was the actions of her peer group – two men who had known each other a long time and who had been in their roles for a while. It was never blatant, but she always felt that she was slightly out of step and that they were reluctant to accept her as an equal. As time went on, the subtle exclusion began to affect her ability to do her work, and in meetings she was presented with decisions that she had played no part in making and which she would have argued against. At first she was convinced that once she had demonstrated that she could do the job well, they would accept her and stop.

They didn't.

So Anna decided that she needed to demonstrate that she wouldn't be shut out and that she wasn't giving in. So the next time that her colleagues went to the bathroom to have a little chat (going to the one place where, as a woman, she couldn't go), she followed them to the door and propped it open so that they couldn't chat without her hearing. The layout of the room meant that there was no invasion of privacy (she'd checked that out with a male colleague) and, in that action, she felt that she had shown that she wasn't going to be the odd one out.

Anna was very apprehensive about her actions, but she felt that she had no choice. Her colleagues were startled by what she did but she justified it by making a joke: 'I was getting worried that something was wrong with one of you: no other men seem to need help so regularly when they go to the loo.'

To be fair to the men, they did laugh, and after that Anna rarely had a problem with them. In time she came to realise that the main protagonist in the behaviour was the less talented one of the men. He had an associate that he had wanted to get her job, and he was not happy about Anna taking it instead, but it wasn't personal animosity towards Anna in particular.

It may be that you aren't the odd one out as a woman. It could be anyone who doesn't meet cultural criteria that have nothing to do with the actual job. Depending on the situation, you can work alongside the way it is or, over time, you can change it.

The chaps were, of course, a bit nonplussed by Anna's action. 'People will see you there, Anna,' they'd banter. 'Yeah, I know, but I don't mind,' she'd reply. She didn't – she was so full of fury that she would stay there for as long as it took to make her point. In the end it took just a few minutes.

The men came out, looked at her, she stared back and it was never mentioned again. She had made her point and, although looking back at it she couldn't quite believe what she'd done, Anna knew that her 'exclusion' was finished. From then on, she has always felt that where she felt left out being the only woman, she now plays to her point of difference. Why be beige when you can be colourful?

Odd one out

On the way up

Anna's insistence at joining her colleagues in the men's bathroom may seem extreme, but it is also brilliant. She broke one of the remaining few taboos in society, and that showed everyone that there was no stopping her. If you are being left out, don't let it lie. Confront it, ideally with humour and always with a little bit of edge.

From the top

This is a workplace not the playground. If team members, whatever their gender, are being excluded from key discussions, then that behaviour needs to be stopped by the leadership.

Use advocates

It is sometimes much better to use your network to work out your problems for you.

Laura is the editor of a tech and gadget magazine. She's worked there for over a decade, and worked her way up so that she knows the business well and has connections throughout the industry. The holding company for the magazine, a flourishing trade specialist publisher, has acquired a new managing director and he has decided to shake things up a bit. Although there's good profitability and stable circulations, clearly, in this time of so much change in media, he should not just let the status quo continue. He calls Laura into his office and says that there is a new role being created of editor-in-chief: does she, as current editor of the magazine, want to apply?

Laura asks what the role entails, and how it is different from her current role. When he answers that there is no editing of the magazine, but more high-level directional supervision, she has doubts about her ability. She has spent years earning the right to call herself one of the best in the business (the magazine has won several awards in its sector). She begins to doubt herself in two ways: first, whether her current skills are transferable to an editor-in-chief role; second, whether she has the capability to learn new skills. As a mother of a young family, has she got the energy for this new role?

This is an altogether too familiar internal conversation. In the end, faced with a twenty-four-hour deadline as to whether to apply (yes, you read that right – just one day), she declines. Someone else from the wider organisation takes the role, and – partly in order to save face – she requests a transfer to another magazine.

Months later, the situation is stark. Laura has done her best in transforming her new magazine, making it more vibrant; but it is a monthly title, not a weekly, and she feels underused. Furthermore, looking back to her previous title, she feels really, really cross. Her successor as editor-in-chief has brought nothing, in her view, to the title. He hasn't delivered an exciting new vision. He does her old job as editor – not a broader, more visionary role. He is less available to her old set of contacts, with whom she has, of course, stayed in touch. She works a four-day week (one of the other reasons that she was concerned about taking the editor-in-chief title). He works a five-day week, but stays in the office more of the time, doesn't stay at evening events and won't spend time making stories; in her view, he just waits for them to arrive. She sees now, very clearly, that he is not any better than she is at the job. He is just much, much, much better at convincing senior management of his skills.

She says of herself: 'I never made the case to my boss that I was the best person for the job. I realise now that in twenty-five years of my working life I have never done this. I sit back, thinking that, of course, everyone knows that I am good. Meanwhile, other people are pushing themselves forward. I was vulnerable. I allowed myself to drift out of the hierarchy at work.'

Laura begins to be very angry. Rather than storm into the situation at work and make demands, she acts on her instincts to gather support and to work it. She begins having quiet drinks with her old contact list. She allows them to tell her how much they miss her, how much they feel that the magazine is not as good as it used to be. She sympathises, but talks up her new job. Talks about how fantastic her new magazine is becoming. She also mentions how many other people have told her how terrible the new editor-in-chief is. She muses that it doesn't seem to be getting back to the management of the holding company. She mentions that her contact is so important, if only he might say something, then that would really create a stir, as it is such a shame to see the magazine, which she still loves, go into a downward spiral, particularly when under her control it was such a champion of the industry sector.

So by networking, by flattering her old contacts, she begins to create a buzz about the uselessness of her successor. Then Laura acts. She takes a big risk, but she feels that continuing as she is doing is out of the question.

Laura goes to see her managing director. She begins by saying how the re-launch of her current magazine has been really well received by its readers. Then she resigns.

She has decided she does not want to go on working for the business in her current role. She wants her old magazine back, or she wants out. She has decided to go freelance as a writer, and has secured a couple of long-term projects. She will have more time for her family and be out of the organisation that has, in her view, overlooked her.

The MD immediately asks for time to consider an alternative role. She ironically gives him twenty-four hours. Her MD has had several weeks of lobbying on her behalf by her old network. This is a people business. The contacts, who are also the people that buy advertising in the title, have no faith in the new editor-in-chief but want Laura back. Within twenty-four hours he offers Laura the editor-in-chief role of her old title, and the pay rise that goes with it.

Laura played the long game here. At no point did she do or say anything to undermine her rival or show her anger publicly. Yes, she was Machiavellian, perhaps, and rather than get involved in a fight, she worked behind the scenes. Laura reclaimed her career. Brilliantly, she manoeuvred the situation to get what she wanted.

ANGER STRATEGY 3

Use advocates

On the way up

Don't be complacent. Don't think that people will know how good you are at your role if you don't keep reminding them. There is a share of voice in play here. Someone is telling the boss how brilliant they are at their job. If it isn't you, then it is someone else.

However, if you are pushed sideways, then you do not have to act in an out-and-out way. You can be subtle and enlist advocates to do the work to redress the situation for you

From the top

Bear in mind that women suffer from entitlement deficit. A man is more likely to be pushing for a bigger role all day, every day. Just because a woman isn't doing so does not mean that you should overlook her for a promotion. As Laura's boss did, if you have made a mistake, undo it.

Go feral

There are those who believe that the office is closer to the jungle than it looks. In order to survive office politics, sometimes you have to make it very clear that you can operate on any level required. However calm and considered your brand image is, you need a reserve of feral behaviour to call upon when you need it. Use your anger about something as inspiration and create a boundary, a line, which those around you fear to cross lightly.

Again, use of anger as a way of drawing a line seems to come more easily to men. It is also more easily forgiven in men: those around them often regard it as a sign of a strong leader and will shrug it off, whereas they will react with more trepidation when faced by female fury. Therefore this is not to be done lightly. Don't throw a temper tantrum every week. But very occasionally let it be known that you are a lioness, not a pussy cat, when provoked.

This is one of those secret tactics that very few successful people, male or female, will admit to. But most, at some stage in their rise up the career ladder, have drawn the line, and have done so emphatically.

Jackie was involved in a new business pitch for a large

project at her medium-size public relations firm. She had worked hard on coming up with a new and original idea for the pitch. This had been part of the written submission, and was under consideration for the formal pitch meeting, together with some other, more business-as-usual ideas. It became clear, as the team were preparing for the meeting, that the consensus in the room was that Jackie's less conventional idea was being left out. Jackie made the argument for its inclusion a couple of times and was met with lukewarm enthusiasm. The rest of the team would not argue against the idea – they had no arguments to counter Jackie's calm and reasoned approach – but nor would they accept it. In the end Jackie asked outright: 'Are you leaving this out?'

All sorts of reasons were given, but the answer was yes. So Jackie threw a tantrum. She stood up, slammed her papers on the table, and said, 'We will not win this pitch on facts alone. This idea is the most emotional sell that we have, and you're leaving it out. I don't know what's wrong with you, but I know this decision is a mistake,' and she swept out of the room.

A couple of hours later, the pitch leader appeared in her office. 'Please, will you come back in and help us work up your idea? We've talked it over and we don't want to leave it out.'

If Jackie threw a tantrum a week, this would never have worked. But sometimes, just occasionally, if you are passionate almost to a violent level, then it will enhance the fact that you care about the business.

Company boss Dina only uses the outburst of passion when it is not directly affecting something she cares about. This means that she can keep it under control. So when, recently, she found herself signing off a redundancy payment for someone who had decided to leave (and whom she did not want to go), she had a full temper fit in the meeting with her inner team about it. 'This was useful for two reasons,' she confides. 'First, it made it clear to the inner team that I would not sign big cheques for people to leave lightly. Second, it showed them that I expected their loyalty personally.' Dina says that she was not really emotionally involved, in this case, with the leaver. It would have been too personal and upsetting if she was. In that moment she showed as much emotion, though, as if she was personally upset, and this gave her the opportunity to draw some lines in case the leaver's behaviour was contagious.

ANGER STRATEGY 4

Go feral

On the way up

Sometimes you need to behave as though you are in the jungle defending your turf. There are a number of ways to do this. You can show your anger. If you are dealing with a power-hungry tiger, then sometimes you need to show your teeth before the battle begins. If you really feel that you are on someone's hit-list, then try one of these tactics: steer them down the wrong channel; enlist support before any meeting begins from the other participants; if you can, use banter to your own advantage – for example, if someone else uses the trick of always sitting next to the boss, make a bit of a joke about it, save them the chair. If all else fails, we have known people who have resolved the situation in a completely different way. Try this: recommend them to a headhunter you can trust.

From the top

Clearly you can't allow decisions to be swayed by individuals having a temper tantrum. However, if this is what valuable team members are driven to, then the lines of communication are not healthy and you need to take action to ensure that apparent consensus among your teams is genuine and not just the behaviour you have asked for in public. A healthy environment for disagreement and resolution is better for long-term success than a team where no one ever argues the point for fear of repercussions.

CASE STUDY 5

Play the long game

Achievement always comes in measured portions when you are at school: you pass exams, you make the grade, you move onwards and upwards. It's all about getting you ready for your first job. After that, you're on your own. Two, ten or twenty years – it's not a plan or a defined path. One recruiter we spoke to said that any candidate saying to them that they had defined goals at set points struck them as inflexible and too linear in their thinking. Today's employers like employees who are open-minded and fluid.

So once you're at work, there are no definitions. One man we spoke to claims that it's all about culture and behaviour, despite what the HR team says. This situation can be difficult to negotiate when you are a woman.

Many women find anger a really awkward emotion. Necks redden, our eyes well up and, even worse, your voice has a tendency to go wobbly just as you're trying to make your point. We lose the impact of our emotion due to the physical manifestations.

If you are a woman with people working for you, it's key to ensure that frustration at any aspect of their work doesn't boil over into a situation that can be dismissed as 'She's in a bad mood, best avoid her.'

On the other hand, don't suppress your humanity too much. It can be hurtful if you discover that you are referred to as an Ice Maiden. (It also provides a useful pigeon-hole to dump you in if you let it define your working style.)

Playing the long game involves you deciding where you'll pick your fights. One woman we spoke to, Gaby, says she doesn't sweat the small stuff. She works for a man who regularly sends aggressive emails and yet is not confrontational in person. 'So if my design team has created something, he will always find a minor fault that he is unhappy with. We once exchanged twenty-four emails about font choice, and he eventually accused me of not being involved enough in my projects. I have four graphic designers working for me, and I have a degree in French and Business. What the hell do I know about which font looks best? We decide on the overall feel and how it meets the brief.'

Gaby knows that this behaviour probably stems from causes completely separate from her and her performance. So she lets this behaviour slide. 'If I got into a fight with him over every little thing, I would be playing his game,' she says. 'Early on, when I saw what he was like, I decided that I would have red lines that I would fight to the end for. Sometimes those fights go on for what feels like ages – a reorganisation that he feels is unnecessary but which I know will be better for my department. For example, I make sure that I have a number of elements I can bring to the skirmishes so that it carries on until I can get my views heard properly. I never take an early refusal on my red-line issues as the end. On other things, I look at the issue in balance and know that I can be flexible on something even if it isn't what I would chose to do. I let him think he's won because I am always thinking about my long game. My husband finds my approach weird, as I can appear to be just rolling over. I just think that as long as I get what I ultimately want, am I really bothered about the little things? As long as my team is happy and rewarded properly and doing great work, it's fine. I'm not going to get my next job on the basis of whether my previous boss chatted about my holiday plans or the football.'

It's always tricky not to let your emotions get the better of you, and heaven knows sometimes it is hard not to take things personally, but if you get the measure of your colleagues you'll know when the long game is the game to play.

ANGER STRATEGY 5

Play the long game

On the way up

Pick your fights. You won't always have a natural empathy with your boss or colleagues. In fact, you are very lucky if you always do. This means, inevitably, that you will not always get the feedback and the endorsement that you might know that you deserve. Do not take your boss up on every single instance of this. Do not sweat the small stuff. Take the long view and consider where and when to show your anger.

From the top

Is one of your team taking things too personally in your view? Of course, you should be tempering every criticism with a pat on the back – that is basic management. But if someone is over-reacting, then some independent coaching might be all they need to gain useful perspective.

Anger in summary

Holding on to your anger is grasping a hot coal with the intent of throwing it at someone else, you are the one who will be burned.

You will not be punished for your anger, you will be punished by your anger.

Bitterness is like cancer. It eats upon the host. But anger is like fire. It burns it all clean.

The first two quotations are from Buddha. The third is Maya Angelou.

The real truth here is that no one thinks that random acts of anger are of any use to you at all. Equally, assuming a demeanour of ladylike calm and acceptance is not always good for you or your career.

There will be things at work that make you angry. The idea that women get pissed off and will do something about it is still apparently a bit of a shock in some professional circles, but not in many. Real anger can get you places if used strategically. It's like a turbocharge for change. Don't lash out wildly. Use your anger to drive your career.

Don't let anger eat you up. Use it.

Anger: The strategies in brief

On the way up

1. Draw the line. If you are undermined in the workplace, get angry, take the power back.
2. If you are excluded, fight your way back in. Refuse to be side-lined. Confront the excluders.

3. Enlist third-party advocates to make your case for you. You should always speak up for yourself, of course, but when things get bad, make sure that you have cultivated the right advocates to speak for you.

4. Use outbursts of passion and anger strategically – they work in two ways if you use them rarely. They have impact from rarity that constant angry outbursts do not, and they develop your reputation for being really passionate about the things you care about: it will warn people off trampling on your boundaries.

5. Pick your fights. Don't sweat the small stuff. Don't forget the things that annoy you, but save your anger for when it will count.

From the top

1. Women are more likely to be conditioned to be agreeable in order to be liked. You might need to give the women who work for you permission to be pissed off and to draw the line.

2. This is a workplace culture issue. Don't let decisions be made when key members of the team are being excluded.

3. Are you overlooking a woman for promotion because she is less likely to ask for it? Listen to those third-party advocates. Seek out their views on your business. You might find their objectivity is useful to you.

4. Obviously, you cannot run a business based on people's temper tantrums. However, the best decisions can sometimes come from disagreements, and it is always good to know what your team are passionate about and who really cares.

5. If team members have problems working through their

disagreements, then some coaching might be necessary so that everyone can operate with the firm's best interests at heart for the long term.

ONE VOICE: GLORIA

Gloria is approaching her sixty-second birthday. She is the managing director of a small business, part of a larger group. She's considering whether to retire, after working without any break for over forty years. She loves her job, although there are aspects of it that have made her angry for some time, and that, enough is enough.

'I will be sixty-two this summer. And I have worked since I was twenty-one. And over that period of time I have seen an awful lot of change particularly, I think, in the way that women are respected in our industry. And in the recognition of the contribution women can actually play. My son was born when I was thirty-six. I had three weeks off, because otherwise we couldn't have paid the mortgage. I feel, quite frankly, that I have had a very long working life, a very enjoyable one. But one without any sustained level of a break to spend with family.

'Part of me now wants to have time for me. Because I have felt, throughout my long, long career, that I have never had "me time". And so, all of a sudden, when you reach a certain age, mortality comes to face you; but moreover I think that I want to have time when I feel young and I feel healthy to enjoy things outside work. I do fear leaving this behind means that I would become very frustrated and bored. Because what keeps my mind fresh and stimulated is my team – the average age of the team is twenty-six, and I feel mentally their age.

'I don't want to be like my friends who don't have that from work. I have seen people who have retired at much younger than me, and I think that they do feel frustrated with not having the stimulus. And equally just even having some kind of routine. Because for many years you're working for four or five days. Your days are very full, but equally you have that sense of achievement at the end of the day or the end of the week or the end of the month, or whatever it might be. And the goals you have actually set yourself. Leaving that, all of a sudden, where are you going to get that sense of achievement from?

And I think that is probably where, at this stage, you feel very wary of making that change. Because you are going to say what is going to replace that sense of achievement, where am I going to get it from? What will keep me fresh in mind and stimulated, and what goal can I set myself outside of work? What I am thinking of doing is charity. Because what I would like to think is that I have got enough drive and skills that maybe I could help other people in a way that I have just been too busy to so far. Literally. Work is work. And that again means that things that I have probably wanted to do outside of work I have never got to do. I know this sounds really silly, but playing golf. I have never been able to find time. Yes, isn't it strange that men find the time to go out and play golf? How can they go on all these golf days? I can't. I could not; I have a strong sense of responsibility. I am constantly amazed by the lack of responsibility that other people have. I always feel that I have fitted my life around business and business has never fitted around me.

'Now it has come to the point where I do actually want to spend more time improving my golf. I do want to spend more time with friends, but I do also want to keep my mind busy and get some new goals. So I am at a bit of a hiatus. Not sure when is the appropriate time to leave and let other people take over, when I would feel that I was not letting anyone down. I think women particularly feel very strongly about that. I think we are very close to the people we work with, and I think this, again, goes back to sense of responsibility, which is very strong in us. So we are the ones who say, "Don't worry about it, we will not go until the team, the company, the whatever it is, is in a good place."

'I have heard of people, men actually more than women, who have retired too early. And they have said to me, "You'll hate it." Because I am quite a high achiever. And they were the same. And a particular friend of mine said, "Do you know what? I just hate being at home." I said, "But surely you've got lots to do?" And he said, "But there's nothing that is replacing that sense of achievement that I used to have at work." He was warning me, and he was saying be really, really careful before you decide to end it for ever. Sounds dreadful, doesn't it?

'His advice was to ease yourself away. And to feel comfortable with the space that you are creating. But I do think that as you grow more mature you make hard decisions better. I really do. And, equally, I think you face up to things far more. There have been issues that have made me think – two things really. The death of a very close friend of mine – well, my best friend – that brings your own mortality quite close. The second thing is that people who you deal with as clients change on a really regular basis. You have to regularly begin again at working at the relationship. Sometimes you think, "I don't know whether I can be arsed to go through this yet again." I have been through it half a dozen times now, and now we've got somebody else that quite frankly knows sweet FA. And they are challenging us, and yet she's talking absolute nonsense.

'I don't know if I can keep my patience any longer. I feel like turning to her and saying, "You start telling me what to do when you understand what we do."

'It really is Groundhog Day. I think that the problem is that it gets harder because they are constantly asking you to reinvent the wheel, but all you are doing is getting an old wheel and slightly adjusting it. And that frustrates me. Really frustrates me because they don't really want a new wheel. They just want the old wheel. Just twiddle with it.

'Yet every appraisal you get, they say, "We would like you to come up with fresh ideas." And you think, I don't believe this. What about this menu of fresh ideas that we gave you and which you said were "Very, very nice, very good, yes we like that"? But then in reality they just go ahead with the old proven ideas.

'So that frustrates me. And so I do think you get to the end of your tether. I have noticed that some of the more recent people have obviously got more patience, because they haven't been through it twenty times.

'Everybody says, "Gloria, you have got more energy than anybody I know." So my energy is still there. I have never let the team down. I still enjoy new business. I get an awful lot of enjoyment out of it.

'I know I could end up on a charity committee that had more of a sense of being like Groundhog Day every time which would drive me mad. I would be like, come on, we have got to change things. I don't like committees if they are not making decisions.

'In terms of work, I have got to start trying to make my own rules. Up until now, work has always given me challenges, and I have always stepped up to the mark – well, I would like to think so. Now, I need to say: this is the bit that I don't want to do. And this is the bit I actually think I can actually help with.

'Because I love being with my team. I love being with my team.

'It's a mix of emotions. Because part of you is quite fearful of what the future holds if something is taken away. Then there's the other side, which excites me. I think a lot of people – I am not one of those – have an idealist vision of what not working can be. I don't. And that's why I want to get it right.'

CHAPTER 7

KARMA

*Women are not in the network of
chaps: how to pay favours forward
and how helping others helps you*

N o, it's not one of those topics that will be at the front
of your mind in any career planning, never mind a job
interview. If, however, the chapter heading had read 'A discussion around causality', you wouldn't be sniffy about this at all.

In fact, Karma does raise interesting questions around
careers. Destiny or free will? Do you roll with the path laid out
for you, or are you more maverick than that? Do we operate in
a vacuum, or is there room for ethics? The principle of Karma
is the law that brings back the results and consequences of
actions to the person performing them.

So what's this got to do with my career? Well, Booz Allen
Hamilton/Aspen Institute evidence shows that companies
that operate a values-driven culture generate a more positive
association among their employees which helps with recruitment and retention.

The three major benefits of active corporate social responsibility (which these days is much more than letting your
employees volunteer for charities – it includes every aspect of
the business's impact on the environment and context within
which they operate) are: it helps others; it helps build better
communities; it helps the bottom line. Adecco in the USA

estimated that 83 per cent of employees prefer to work for a company that supports causes or charities.

It also helps companies get increased name recognition and reputation among consumers – so employees get a nice 'glow' when they say where they work. Corporate sponsored volunteering experiences are shown to result in reported higher job satisfaction and a greater commitment to the company, as well as making employees believe that the volunteering helps them to develop their skills and leadership potential.

So good Karma is good business all round.

Individual Karma also creates a circle of reward. Or not, depending on how you play it. Talk to anyone who has been between roles with no clear destination, and they will all remember the people who dropped them. They recall the invitations – even just for a cup of tea or coffee – that get cancelled via email with no covering note. You are invisible until you get a new job.

Your individual behaviour should be based on treating people the way you'd like to be treated. Call it Karma, causality, whatever … It matters.

CASE STUDY 1

Always on

In recent years there has been an increasing amount of focus on Emotional Intelligence Quota (EQ) as being of equal importance to IQ. Great teams don't just appear as a result of the collective intelligence of the people within them: it's key that the blend of people and their personalities is right. The phrase 'all of us together is better than one of us alone' is written on the wall of a company and pretty much sums up the collective nature of work at that organisation.

There are very few places where the reclusive genius flourishes long-term, or where it's effective to just turn on the magic when your boss appears. Lucy Kellaway, a columnist with the *Financial Times*, recently put out a podcast where she talked about how people behave in reception. This review was sparked by the news that a property development company asked their receptionist to give feedback on how visitors behaved when they arrived: the minute the person got in the lift, she called the chief executive. In a world where big deals are initially confirmed by a handshake, character is key.

It is surprising that people are unaware of how they interact with others. Failing to make eye contact, scanning the room for the next person they need to network with (if you say to your current contact, 'I'm sorry, I am due to find X, please excuse my looking around for them', that's OK; staring over someone's shoulder twitchily isn't). If a receptionist or security guard says, 'Good Morning' to you, you should always respond. Grumpily looking at your mobile phone and grunting is the sign of someone who doesn't understand that you are always on. Like Lucy, we have witnessed people who don't realise that reception is a bit of a showcase – you don't know who else is there. You create your initial personal brand impression by the way you behave and remember: you are always on.

The 'always on' extends from reception, though. While not expecting mindless smiling and automatic 'have a nice day' responses, being your best self is worthwhile. One of us once inherited a team member who announced that they weren't a morning person and that they couldn't be expected to talk to anyone before 10.30. She was seriously grumpy and unhelpful if approached before then. In the end she left the organisation as it was unfair that her colleagues had the choice of hanging around until she was ready to interact with them or having her presence sitting at her desk looking as if she'd rather be taking out her own teeth with pliers than be there. Yes, she was working (on anything that wasn't interacting at a personal level, i.e., emails and documents), but there was no consideration for colleagues and their needs at all.

Although this book is about being the best you can be, it isn't just about you. It's also the impression you make and the feelings you engender in your colleagues and peers.

So many times, people have come away from a meeting thinking that they have seriously messed up with their boss or a colleague because they are rude and abrupt. It poisons the atmosphere, and the next encounter is overshadowed by the resonance of the last one. If you're the one who has been abrupt, you will sense that change and maybe hold back as the other person seems on edge with you – and so it continues.

Jamie once worked with a female boss with whom she loved to work. They made a great team, and when she went on maternity leave she genuinely missed her. When she came back, it was even better than before and they swept all before them. Six months in, though, and she became aware that she was less open to her ideas, and was less enthusiastic about the work. She started to get worried, as she had thought that they were a great team. She was out with her elder sister one night and she confided in her. 'She's exhausted,' her sister replied, 'I bet her baby isn't sleeping and your place is so full-on that she thinks she can't say.'

Sensitively, Jamie brought up the topic one day when they were on the way back from a meeting. Away from the office it was less emotionally loaded, and finally her boss said that for the last four months she hadn't slept more than three or four hours a night.

If you are always on, so are your boss and your colleagues. It would do us all a lot of good if we remembered the impact we have when we forget that the people that we work with are human too.

Always on

On the way up

When you are in the workplace, you're on. There is no down time. If you're in a career hurry, you need to bear this in mind in the bar after work as well. You are being judged, and people will give you brownie points for how you behave around them and detract points too. There's no such thing as down time with your colleagues, even if you think there is.

From the top

There's an old saying that you should be careful how you treat people on your way up the ladder as they may pass you on your way down. Hopefully your career ascent will continue unabated, but you might want to bear in mind that someone who works for you today may some day be your boss. The other truth is that if you're brusque or casual with someone you encounter – maybe you just haven't got time for that cold call today, or you need your PA to put someone off for months because you're too busy – that person will remember you. Always. We can guarantee that.

Be your best self

It would surprise you to know who Daisy, a business writer, works for. The reputation of the organisation is for fairness, for democratic values, as a champion of women's rights. Daisy's experiences were of these values, until two things happened at about the same time. First of all, she became more senior in her role and, due for promotion, she was made chief writer of her section. Second, she became pregnant. As far as Daisy is concerned, it was as if she had changed overnight. During the period leading up to her maternity leave she lost status and was noticeably undermined at the expense of more junior men. When, after giving birth to a gorgeous baby girl, she got in touch with her boss to arrange a meeting to discuss how and when she'd come back to work, he didn't turn up. He completely missed the appointment. Finally, the meeting took place and a period in her working life began that Daisy describes as 'hellish'. Four weeks after going back to work, she was called into a disciplinary meeting. When she asked for specifics about her decline in performance, her boss could come up with nothing stronger than supposedly 'inappropriate feature ideas'.

She sought out the most senior woman manager, a champion of women's equality at work. One of the most depressing aspects of Daisy's recent experiences was that this woman gave her absolutely no support. 'If it were me in that position of strength,' Daisy explains, 'I would take that woman by the hand and march her to senior management and insist that they look after her.' Daisy has gone from being a key player to a nonentity. No one has stood up for her throughout the organisation. The situation is ongoing, as her employers are probably expecting her to have another baby. She might, she might not – but either way her loyalty to them has been out of proportion to how she has been treated. What a shame that no one opted to be their best self in her organisation and to help her out. If her loyalty has been firm despite all the knock-backs, only imagine how it would be for her employers if someone senior had acted with even a hint of good Karma.

The organisation that Daisy works for is not filled with good Karma. The senior management are not doing their best for the people who need championing, and this sadly will apply irrespective of gender or circumstance. This particular organisation has been flat-lining in business terms for some time. Although it may not be obvious, the long-term success of any business is dependent on having a culture of positivity. It is not something that a business consultant can quantify, but it is something that every successful business head understands at some level. You can have an organisation that is built on everyone taking advantage of everyone else's weakness. Or you build a business where everyone gives everyone else a leg up. For this to work you need a flow, from the top, of good Karma. Everyone needs to be what successful entrepreneur, designer and iconoclast Vivienne Westwood would call 'your best self'. Speaking in the summer of 2013, Westwood said that at every point of our lives there are two possible ways to act. One is that dictated by 'the ordinary self' and driven by immediate gratification. The other is your 'best self'. We all have one, and we all know exactly what it would tell us to do. If we take a breath and listen to that self, then we enter into a world where Karma prevails.

Baroness Helena Kennedy is one of the most successful and high-profile women in law in the UK. Throughout her forty-year career she has seen improvements for women in work. But she still sees very real hurdles. 'The pace of change isn't good enough' is her main verdict. She believes that there's less nurturing of younger women and always has been. 'Men tend to nurture and promote younger men. It's an instinctive thing; you recognise your younger self and make opportunities available.' As there are fewer senior women in business, this tends to happen less for junior women, and so the traditional shape of senior management is self-perpetuating. There may, in addition, be the worry of seeming to favour young women if you are a man. How does it look if you take them to lunch, and for private coaching meetings? Instead, it seems to Kennedy as if men are virtually cloning themselves, replacing themselves with younger versions of themselves, in business and in politics as well as law.

It is not men at the top who are limiting women's careers, in her view; it is middle-management men. They're struggling to climb the promotion ladder themselves and have no interest in supporting anyone, but particularly women, who – as we have discovered (think back to the survey in the introduction, in particular) – can seem less predictable to them and harder to read.

Baroness Kennedy's solution is simple. Build the promotion of diversity into the key performance indicators of anyone in middle management. Judge them on what they have done to find successors that are women, or from an ethnic minority. She believes that this is much fairer than quotas. It seems an elegant solution. Don't count on people being their 'best self'. Make fairness in supporting their team an essential and declared part of how they are judged.

KARMA STRATEGY 2

Be your best self

On the way up

Daisy's employers have exploited her loyalty to the business. Daisy has been her best self. Her employers have not reciprocated. She should explain this to them, to see if they can change, or she should leave for another culture, where the corridors run not with self-interest but with positivity.

From the top

Karma starts and ends at the top. It is crucial to a successful culture in any sector. Senior managers must think and act as their best selves. Try mandating fairness in your middle managers' KPIs.

CASE STUDY 3

Make a memory

Our work weeks have a certain pattern and rhythm. Your weekly meeting with the team is always on Tuesday at ten o'clock; as month end approaches, people panic about getting tasks done – you know the routine.

Routine is a reassuring thing, in a way. Most people don't live their work lives in a series of high-adrenaline, heart-pumping adventures. Even stuntmen do weeks and months of detailed, quite low-profile tests and calculations before they throw themselves off buildings or take part in a high-speed chase.

It's a common error to think that a couple of high-profile 'wins' can push your career to new heights. Those big bangs normally either reinforce a view of you or lead to a reappraisal. If you're someone who normally coasts along and then claims the big project win as your own on a regular basis, in time that will be the perception of you. The view will be: able to deliver the deal but ultimately all about themselves.

Similarly, if you're uneasy in the limelight but are world-class when it comes to planning and delivery, don't assume that those qualities aren't valued where you work (assuming you don't work in logistics). Be aware of your talents and qualities and decide what you want to be known for – what the memory of you will be.

At a time when business was tough, Clare knew that the pay rise wasn't going to be big. In fact, it was likely that unless business picked up, people would lose their jobs. She decided that she liked where she worked, that she'd stick with the company and that the memory that she'd create would stand her in good stead a few months down the line. Her boss didn't pull any punches when he talked about how things were. He told Clare that her pay would be going up a nominal amount and that recruitment was frozen. If people left, they weren't going to be replaced. Clare had expected this and was a bit worried that it would mean she'd be doing even more work with fewer resources.

However, she had a few thoughts about how some small elements of the department's work could be done more efficiently, and she'd written them down. She pushed the piece of paper across the table and said she'd be happy to talk about her ideas. That if things changed and she achieved certain goals, she might get another chance to talk about her package. The paper went to the bottom of the pile, and she decided that it was probably irrelevant. There were too many bigger things going on, probably. Clare had made her point, in the best way, and put it in writing, too, to refer back to later.

By not claiming that this situation was more personally upsetting for her than any of her colleagues or threatening to quit, Clare created a memory. It was the memory of someone who could see the bigger picture and contribute.

No one can be automaton-like in the way they work, but by consistently thinking about the memory we're going to create – the way colleagues would sum you up in a sentence, for example – we can create a perception that works for us. Most people interact with dozens of people a day, and it can all blur into one. Make sure that you are memorable for all the right reasons.

Make a memory

On the way up

You can be extraordinary in very ordinary situations. Particularly, as we have seen here, where Clare's boss was expecting a bad meeting about a pay freeze, and she confounded his expectations in a way that was extremely memorable. A small act of gracefulness, of generosity, or of compassion can brand you as someone people want to have in their team.

From the top

People have a set of expectations about bosses. If you can confound them – by breaking with protocol, by picking up details, by acts of kindness and warmth – then you will earn their loyalty. Sue can remember walking back to her old offices with then UK MD Nick Lawson (now MediaCom EMEA CEO). There was dog mess on the steps. Exceptionally large and unpleasant. 'I'll get someone to clean that up,' she said. 'No,' Nick replied, 'I'll clear it up … I'm not asking anyone who works for me to do something that I wouldn't do myself.' No one apart from them saw what happened. Nick wasn't demonstrating good leadership for an audience. He's just a great leader. And he made a memory.

Pay it forward

Madeleine Albright is often quoted as saying that there is a special place in hell for women who don't help other women. This maybe comes from the lack of female networks that exist but, actually, help should be gender-neutral. It is always better if it isn't self-serving too.

If you have something that might help someone else – a book, a name, an experience, that might benefit them – give it freely. Don't save up your favours for when you'll get a quick payback; play the long game.

The other thing about paying it forward is to keep your word. If you're going to introduce people via email, then do it. If you've said you'll do it and then have second thoughts, ask the person who is the focus of the introduction if it's OK. If they say no, then write a holding note about the contact being really busy at the moment and defer the introduction. That way you keep both people happy and your credibility in place. If they say yes, then get on with it and just leave them to sort themselves out.

Don't be afraid to ask people what it is they really want. You don't want to be the person who forced a colleague to sit through three hours of someone's life story when you thought it was just a cup of coffee.

One of the most successful people we know excels at bringing people together and easing the path of projects, ideas and colleagues. They understand that a quick email or note asking how things are is a fast and painless way of keeping momentum and warmth in a situation. Phoning people might feel more immediate but can seem intrusive and inappropriate. You don't want to be the person whose message is deleted as soon as your number is recognised.

Maya was in her late twenties when she was appointed to the board at work. Immediately her unofficial mentor Esther, a much more senior woman who had been keeping an eye on her and helping to promote her interests in a largely masculine boardroom, took her for dinner. 'Let me give you some advice,' Esther said over a glass of celebratory champagne. 'Don't be surprised if you now feel awful about work.' Maya was surprised at what her friend was saying. She'd worked so hard for the promotion that she felt was so deserved. This, as she went on to explain, was exactly Esther's point. 'You've been working towards this role for so long. You think that you are already doing most of it. It may take you three to six months to understand exactly what a board director does that isn't just in a list of tasks. My experience is that you may well feel disillusioned and empty that there is not a sudden change in your status, or indeed in the respect that you receive from the rest of the workplace. I want you to be warned. I went through a huge disillusionment after my first big promotion, and it was a shock. You're going to have a brilliant career. This is your first big step up the ladder. Don't worry if it takes a few weeks, even months, to catch on.'

Esther's advice to Maya was timely, and in the spirit of paying it forward. She didn't need to share her personal experiences with her. Arguably, she'd already done enough. She'd already represented her and pushed for her promotion. This now was an extra kindness, a bit of shared experience that would make life easier and smoother during the transition in status.

There are those who believe that there is no such thing as good leadership without paying it forward. Certainly a good culture has the seeds in it of everyone paying it forward where they can, offering their help, even when they are busy, in the knowledge that people will offer to help them in return when they need it.

Pay it forward

On the way up

If you have something that will help someone else, then pay it forward. Don't negotiate over it. Don't keep it behind for when you need a favour. Your generosity will not have a guaranteed return from the person that you have helped. But the culture that you are helping to create or to sustain at work will benefit you and the organisation. This could be as easy as a piece of unsolicited advice that you wish you had received, or as concrete and anonymous as bringing in cakes to the office kitchen.

From the top

It is one thing to grant favours to people when they ask for your help. It is another to create an atmosphere of general paying it forward, where favours are not exchanged in some kind of barter or loan system (perhaps with interest). Where, instead, positive actions are undertaken generously, where something great happens and, because you don't know who did you that favour, you simply do one for someone else. If you can create that kind of environment, then your talent will hate to leave, and the positive Karma you establish will give you a competitive advantage.

CASE STUDY 5

We're all human

Well, that states the obvious. Yet some women in the workplace overlook the human factor because they are so keen to prove themselves. If you are trying to be superwoman yourself, then other people's very human characteristics may just seem irrelevant. If this strikes a chord, then you may be missing out on plain acts of common humanity that could help your career.

Elizabeth isn't happy. She has yet another meeting with the most unpopular client in the whole agency. She works at a media planning agency, and the client in question, a car hire firm, is led by a middle-aged man, clearly past his career peak, who either cannot or will not make decisions. When he does, he goes back on them. The last time she produced an email minuting his decisions, he sent it straight back, cc-ing her boss, with one word in capitals: 'NO.' She has not come to terms yet with this: she hates being undermined, and she hates it when her attention to detail is challenged, because she has the best attention to detail of anyone she has worked with.

Also, the meeting is far from the office, on Friday afternoon, and it is raining. Off she goes. She's unaware that her career is about to change fundamentally for ever (and for the better).

Joining her at this meeting is the account director from the creative agency, Graham. She is expecting to grind through detailed plans for regional and direct mail advertising. Instead, Graham hijacks the meeting. 'I'd like to play you a video,' he says. Logging on to YouTube, he calls up a memorable sporting moment and projects it on to the big screen.

'Until this moment everyone knew that the way to do the high jump competitively was to straddle or scissor the bar. After this moment, which uniquely added inches to the record, the game was changed for ever.' Graham then played the video of Dick Fosbury's record-breaking backward 'Flop' over the bar.

'The work we have been doing for you so far has just been more of the same. I'd like us to do something that will change the game: let us, Elizabeth and me, work together on a plan that will allow you to break all the records in your industry.'

At that moment, tedium left the room and was replaced by excitement, possibilities and potential.

Afterwards, on the train back to London, Elizabeth asked Graham how he turned the meeting around. Basically she asked him how he was so good at his job. He replied simply, 'I never forget that the client is a human being too.'

Since this meeting neither does Elizabeth. She understands Graham's point. We are all human. And we all want to be a bit of a hero. It is a natural human trait. Just like everyone else, her client also wanted to be the hero in a story. He didn't get his kicks from undermining her. He was irritated by her boredom with the account and wasn't about to let her get away with it. Change the atmosphere, as Graham brilliantly did, and positivity will be contagious.

Graham and Elizabeth never did do any paradigm-shifting work on that account. There was no Fosbury Flop in the car-hire marketing plan. The meetings became more fun and more full of potential, however, and everyone bonded over the chance, the hope of change.

Elizabeth learned a valuable lesson. Don't see the people in your meetings as your opponents, or blockages in your way. Look at them as human beings. With hopes, with fears, with a different perspective from yours.

Later in her career she was asked to take a meeting with the creative agency head of a huge multinational account that she was pitching for. She had met him before on another occasion. He had spent the occasion ignoring her in favour of the men in the room or, when forced to interact, patronising her. She was dreading the meeting. She had no hope of positive advice coming her way. She expected to get so cross that there would be complaint. She thought back to Graham and the Fosbury Flop lesson. When the meeting began, she opened with this: 'Before we begin, can I just say how very well you're looking; have you recently been on holiday?'

The meeting, which she had been dreading, couldn't have gone better. The creative agency head made a point of emailing Elizabeth's boss to say how great she was. One opening compliment changed the tone of the whole meeting.

Everyone can be prone to think that what they put the effort into is the most crucial part of the job. Elizabeth wasn't clashing with people that were stupid or annoying, as she had believed. She was clashing with people who had a different set of priorities.

We all have a strong innate desire to be the hero or the heroine of our particular stories. In the last century Joseph Campbell published a book called *The Hero with a Thousand Faces*, which described the 'monomyth': a hero's journey that repeats throughout history in stories told by different cultures around the world. Most successful movies or TV shows tell a version of the story. If you can help someone at work find a way to be the hero or heroine of the day, even in a small and trivial way, then you're giving them hope, potential and enjoyment. You're creating good Karma and a much stronger likelihood that they will, in turn, support you and your ideas (and your career path). We cannot expect to bond instinctively with everyone. However, if you can forge a bond on a human level with those who appear to be in your way, then your journey up the career ladder will be much smoother as a result.

KARMA STRATEGY 5

We're all human

On the way up

Turn a difficult personal relationship into a positive one by complimenting those who you think are in your way or – even better – by crafting a story that they can be the hero or heroine of. They're not there to stand in your way. But they will only help you if you make them feel good, even great, if they do help you out.

From the top

We ask different things from different people at work. Those who work for us may succeed at tasks up to a certain point by being administratively efficient or buttoned down. Others may succeed by being the fun one in the team. As those people progress, they may need help with understanding each other's strengths and weaknesses. Top managers will remember that everyone is a human being. Compassion about each other's strengths and weaknesses may not come naturally to everyone. Bear in mind that your team might need this explaining more than once, and have the patience to spell it out for them.

Karma in summary

Silicon Valley author Guy Kawasaki says that there are only two kinds of people in business: pie bakers and pie eaters. The pie eaters think that there's just one size of pie. If you take a bigger slice, there is less left for them. They spend a lot of time, a huge amount of time, worrying about their share of the pie. You can see those people around you every day at work. Then there are the pie bakers. They don't worry about what size their slice of pie is. They aren't watching what size of pie you're getting compared to them. They are too busy baking a bigger pie for everyone.

It is a lot easier to live in a state of positive Karma to those around you if you believe in the bigger pie. Frankly, so much negative energy is taken up by worrying about whether other people are better off, happier or more liked by the boss that if you give that up – if you can focus instead on positivity to those around you – you'll have more good energy to drive your career. Just try it. If you ever think that your progress at work only comes if others fail, then try to stop. Instead, think about how you can help others. This will mean that they will try to help you back (that's human nature), and it means that you will be making a positive contribution to the workplace overall, if only by creating a more generous atmosphere at work.

It is easy to get confused signals from other people. When we are left out of a meeting that we think we should have been invited to, it can feel like a huge slur. A deliberate insult. Or, it could be a mistake. You'll be happier and have a more productive outcome if you behave as though it is a mistake and not an insult. Try simply saying to the meeting organiser that you wish you had been included, and you would like to be next time, if possible, for these (specific) reasons. But say it with a smile on your face. And make those reasons helpful.

If someone asks you if you're busy, do you always say yes, very busy? Try saying that of course you will make time to help if you are needed. The help will be reciprocal the next time you need some. If you don't, it won't.

If a colleague shouts or creates a bad atmosphere, try being compassionate and offering to help them. It is all too easy to fall into the trap of stereotyping the office grump or tyrant. Be the one that sees through the surface and helps to create a better vibe.

Karma: The strategies in brief

On the way up

1. Always on. There is no down time – you're always being

judged by colleagues. You need to bring your positive self every day.

2. Be your best self. But make sure that you're treated with appreciation by your managers. If not confront them. Or move on.

3. Make a memory. Be extraordinary in even very ordinary situations. You will have an impact.

4. Pay it forward. If you have something that will help someone, then pass it on. Don't wait for a favour that you need to negotiate over. Get some good Karma in the bank.

5. We're all human. Colleagues, customers, clients, they're not there to stand in your way. Make them the hero or heroine of the situation and reap the benefits of that positivity.

From the top

1. Always on. The person you treat brusquely may be a brief forgotten encounter to you, but they will remember you. Always.

2. Mandate fairness in your middle managers' key performance indicators – they should know that it is crucial to their successful career progression to be fair to their teams, not just to deliver short-term results.

3. Make memory. If you break protocol as the boss, it will mean a huge amount to your team.

4. Pay it forward. Always do what you can, not just because it helps the business, but because it will create the kind of atmosphere that everyone will benefit from, and the best people will hate to leave.

5. We're all human. We all need compassion when we are under stress. Set a standard of good intentions in the workplace.

ONE VOICE: CARYS

Carys is a well-respected chief executive who is known for being unfailingly generous and kind. Her generation of women leaders have sometimes had a reputation for being more like men than men in order to get ahead. Carys has climbed every step of the career ladder with a focus on Karma. With one exceptional time which she learned from (as we will here), she has been relaxed, mindful and enjoyed the journey and what she has achieved along the way. She reflects here on following your heart and the one thing she perhaps wishes she had done differently on reflection.

'Yes, I became a director in 1989, and there had only been one other woman director before then. Alpha males wanted to be on the board always, and got the board positions and kept them for forty years. I actually never wanted to be in this industry. There's something about being casual about it, not too pushy. I've never applied for a job. I've never wanted another job than the one I've got. Part of me looks back and thinks there were some other brilliant women I worked with who were conventionally attractive and were forced into a certain role. I was never conventionally attractive … I don't know if that's true or not. I never agonised about it, I just got on and did a good job as far as I saw it and, wherever possible, tried to make it a better job.

'Above all, I am authentic. I would say that what I do is the Shit Sandwich. I'm quite nice to people, I try and be understanding and empathetic and listen, but it doesn't stop me from confronting what's wrong. Nice, and then I'll be horrible. But then I'll say I love you, let's have lunch. I get furious, but then I say, it's only work, there are important things, let's make friends. Is that a feminine thing? I don't know. I think in my early life I suffered from wanting to be liked too much. I think it's a curse for women.

'Before I was promoted I was happy. Suffered for working for an incompetent man, because I wanted to be liked. Rather than complaining, I was too obedient for two years. Trying to make him look good. Trying to cover up cracks, and making others look good.

'Fear of failure is a tremendous problem for women, isn't it? Until we're absolutely certain of every fact. We have to learn to just jump a bit.

'I wanted to be liked, but I didn't want to be one of them. Why would I? I didn't admire most of them – a few of them, but not most of them. I certainly didn't want to be one of them.

'The first company I worked at, there were already senior women, and there were lots of beautiful women there. The other cliché you get is the mother thing. If I'm not the whore, I'm the mother. I object to that really. It's characterised as being mothering. I would hope anybody running large teams of people would be concerned for their welfare. It's the way you run a business ... But having big tits and a big arse you end up being motherly. And I'm not! It's just stereotypes, isn't it?

'I really flowered through work eventually. I moved to a little start-up that became really successful. Bits of me that hadn't been used – the thinking and creative bits – became prized in their own right.

'People said you're mad, taking this ridiculous demotion. You've gone to this little start-up. People were concerned about status, but I wasn't. I'd won that race, and I thought it was pretty worthless. What's the point of sticking around?

'I thought, I'll go and have some more interesting times. I'd always believed in the start-up's mission. The team convinced me it was important to believe in the product, and I'm prone to wanting to believe in something. And they needed a grown-up person to be a director, and they said we want someone like you. So I did it, and it was brilliant fun.

'I have to have something to believe in. If I haven't got a purpose, then what is the point?

'My worst career moment was in the 1990s, when I was just

working to make money. I couldn't keep on doing that, I had to leave. The period when I was just focused on profit was a terrible time of my life. It was three years of utter hell.

'Although I expressed unhappiness, I didn't feel powerful enough to make it stop happening. At the start-up I felt more powerful. I would do it through a third party, but I thought it was important to be powerful. That's how I prefer to do it, through a third party. Most of my life I've been influential but never really been powerful. Women should have that. To be powerless is utterly hideous. Why shouldn't we want to be powerful? Having the power to do positive things is wonderful. I hate that most of my life I've had to do it through a third party. That's when women get labelled devious and manipulative, because they don't confront things head-on, they tend not to have power. The people that are unfairly called manipulative and devious are women and children.

'Motherhood is interesting. I just can't bear all these well-meaning people saying we need to make it possible for an employee to be a working mother. We need to make it possible for everybody to be working PARENTS. We need to make business human. I just think it's doing the worst possible thing to make women a special case. The world has got to have children. Let's just make it possible for people to have children. And dads will like being a better dad, and kids will get to know their dad better. I was lucky to have a husband who was happy to be more than an equal sharer. Let's just de-gender it. And being old. I'm sixty, which is quite old – isn't it? – to keep working. That's about loving what you do.

'People say I'm quite funny. My MD and I just slag each other off the whole time. It's a comedy routine. She moans about me, and I take the piss out of her shoes. I think probably when I was in a more blokey workplace that, even though when I didn't do the drinking and the football, taking the piss was the only thing that made me slightly matey etc. I don't think women don't tell jokes, though, they're just funny. Men tell jokes, they want to be centre-stage. But being funny

… I don't think I've ever told a joke in my life. I'm very analytical … too many facts, not enough room for a gag. If I reflect, I would say, "Tell fewer things better, with a gag."'

AFTERWORD

We embarked on this book with one aim: to ensure that the gender divide in career progression ends, and ends now. This is the time. No business will disagree with the idea that there should be a significant representation of women in senior management. No individual will disagree with the idea that everyone should be able to fulfil their career ambitions regardless of their gender.

Yet companies are still struggling to show gender equality at senior levels. Our own research shows that across the UK, Russia and the USA more than a third of women in employment believe that their gender is holding back their success.

This does not have to be the case. The strategies in this book can turn the situation around and can transform apparent barriers into levers for success.

There needs to be a change in approach both from business leaders and from people on the way up in their careers.

On the way up: if you feel that your career is stalling, don't bemoan the situation. Don't worry about being stuck. It doesn't matter if it is unfair or unreasonable. What matters is to diagnose the situation from a business-only perspective, to adapt to the situation and to work out which of the strategies in these pages you need to adopt in order to come out winning.

From the top: business leaders need to wake up to the fact that they need to change their approach to succession management significantly if they are to retain and to benefit from talented women. It is not enough to maintain that you have created a level playing field if that level playing field does not take into account the differences between men and women that we've talked about in this book: whether that is around the approach to the care of young children or an attitude to banter in the office. If you don't have gender equality in senior management – and very few businesses currently do – then your culture needs to change in order to allow it.

At the beginning of our book we asked you to place yourself on a scale of 1 to 10, where 1 is very feminine and 10 is very masculine, in terms of your style and approach at work. We've been fortunate in that Lightspeed GMI have conducted this survey across professionals in three different countries – the UK, the USA and Russia – and details can be found in the appendix of this book. For your reference, before we go into the results and what they mean, both Sue and Kathryn would place themselves at a 6 or 7. And both Sue and Kathryn have men as colleagues who would be extremely surprised that they were anything higher than a 3 or 4.

Across all three markets men nearly always place themselves at 5 or more: the idea that they might have feminine attributes in their work style is anathema. Women do predominantly place themselves in scores of 1 to 4, but not nearly as exclusively. In fact, 35 per cent of British women score themselves 5+ (i.e., more towards the masculine spectrum), 23 per cent of American women do the same, and so do 40 per cent of Russian professional women.

So what? First, it goes to show that there may be a divide between how you see yourself and how your boss sees you. Second, women are far more adaptable: we can adopt masculine attributes and use them to our advantage much more easily than men can do the opposite. For decades now, we will sometimes wear trousers to work but we've never yet been in a meeting in the UK with a man in a dress or skirt.

The Lightspeed survey reveals other interesting differences, both between men and women and between the nations. In the UK and Russia men are significantly more ambitious than women. This is less true in the USA. Furthermore, 70 per cent of women in the UK and the USA share a belief that there are more barriers to career progression for women than there are for men, but in Russia only 14 per cent of women agree. Overall, and rather sadly in our view, the proportion of both genders who believe they've picked the wrong career is too high – around half agree; perhaps this too is related to strategies for career progression. A point comes when being good at your job is simply not enough, when the strategies to succeed described in these pages – which might feel like they aren't obvious and which you won't get training in – are very necessary to overcome a career blockage. These strategies do work.

For businesses to succeed, things need to change. For personal satisfaction things need to change. Follow these strategies; adapt and win; smash the glass wall; attain the career you deserve.

41 STRATEGIES FOR SUCCESS

On the way up

1. Ask for what you want. Ask for the help you need.

2. Look at how the men around you behave. Don't let yourself be left behind because they self-promote more aggressively than you do.

3. If you feel that your career path is blocked, if you feel that things aren't fair, or aren't moving quickly enough, then break the rules.

4. If someone puts barriers in your way, use them as a leaping-off point. Use the energy that anger gives you to propel you towards your objective.

5. Feel the fear, but do it anyway. Don't let nerves put you off.

6. Be careful where you go. As an individual, it's tempting to see the next big move (or any move) as the answer to issues with your current role. It's key that you make sure that your expectations are in line with where you plan to work.

7. Borrowed brilliance from another category or field is a great, relatively simple way of injecting creative thinking.

8. If everyone is heading in one direction and has a single consensus – go the other way. When they all zig, you should zag.

9. There are many things to fear in life. Failure in a meeting

is not one of them. Expect to fail sometimes, intend to fail sometimes. If you don't, you're never going to learn anything.

10. Push the idea till it breaks.

11. Be naïve, ask the stupid questions, listen to your gut instinct.

12. Build your own personal brand. Work out the right image for you and then look, sound and act the part.

13. Speak their language (even if it's 'football').

14. Be funny. Use humour to lighten the atmosphere. Store up a selection of jokes and deploy them at will. Too much seriousness implies a lack of confidence.

15. Cutting through as an introvert requires hard work. You do not need to take a huge leap out of your comfort zone, but you will need to find a way to extend it on your own terms.

16. Manage upwards and across. This is your responsibility too.

17. Stand up for your ideas. Don't allow the need to be liked to prevent you from being effective.

18. Be seen – make sure that you are visible.

19. If you get yourself into trouble, stick to your principles and keep going to get yourself out of it. Don't put the brakes on, accelerate.

20. If you don't like the tone of the banter around you, do something about it. It's a good idea to give as good as you get. If the situation needs escalation, then don't hesitate to seek formal support to stop it dead.

21. If you do do something you wish could stay private, and it doesn't, either brazen it out or deny. The best tactic is: JDDI (Just Don't Do It).

22. If you need mentoring, find a mentor who has nothing to do with your past or, in fact, your present.

23. Never deviate from your true self.

24. If you can't win the fight, it may be better to give way for now.

25. Don't drown in any work crisis – it isn't worth it. Walk away from a no-win situation sooner rather than later, while you can extract yourself with dignity.

26. If you are undermined in the workplace, get angry, take the power back.

27. If you are excluded, fight your way back in. Refuse to be side-lined. Confront the excluders.

28. Enlist third-party advocates to make your case for you. You should always speak up for yourself, of course, but when things get bad, make sure that you have cultivated the right advocates to speak for you.

29. Use outbursts of passion and anger strategically – they work in two ways if you use them rarely. They have impact from rarity that constant angry outbursts do not, and they develop your reputation for being really passionate about the things you care about – it will warn people off trampling on your boundaries.

30. Pick your fights. Don't sweat the small stuff. Don't forget the things that annoy you, but save your anger for when it will count.

31. Plan your requests. Make your arguments for the benefit of the business, not just your personal benefit.

32. Know when to stop putting up with things. Draw a line, and stick to it. Always.

33. Make sure that you're playing by the unwritten rules of

the business, not just the stated ones. If you think that there aren't any then think again. You just don't know what they are.

34. Play the numbers game. If you hear a 'no' the first time you ask for something, don't see that as the end. Keep asking.

35. Have a playbook of tactics to use in difficult times. If you have a resource to fall back on, you will feel braver and are less likely to react inappropriately.

36. Fight to always have perspective.

37. There is no down time – you're always being judged by colleagues. You need to bring your positive self every day.

38. Be your best self. But make sure that you're treated with appreciation by your managers. If not confront them. Or move on.

39. Make a memory. Be extraordinary in even very ordinary situations. You will have an impact.

40. Pay it forward. If you have something that will help someone, then pass it on. Don't wait for a favour that you need to negotiate over. Get some good Karma in the bank.

41. We're all human. Colleagues, customers, clients, they're not there to stand in your way. Make them the hero or heroine of the situation and reap the benefits of that positivity.

From the top

1. Beware the Peter Principle, and be aware that you might need to explain and encourage team behaviour.

2. Make sure that you encourage the women in your team to have a structured opportunity every month to tell you what they've achieved.

3. As a manager, you have to be able to spot talent, even if it comes in an unconventional form.

4. If unconscious gender bias is going on in your business, then it needs to be uncovered. If fewer women are making progress than men, then frankly it probably means that this is the case.

5. Take the time to spot talent. If you can't see the talent in the quieter people – often that means the women – then slow down, try harder, look deeper.

6. If you're making ambitious hires, know that you have the scope to deliver on your promises.

7. Encourage everyone in the team to think of themselves as creative. Don't let it be owned by an elite team – bring out the creativity in everyone.

8. If there is a consensus that is sweeping everyone in an unchallenged direction, encourage the lone voice that puts forward another point of view and hear what they have to say before signing off for the majority decision.

9. Encourage the team to believe that they have permission to screw things up sometimes. An environment where no one ever fails means an environment that stifles any creative leaps.

10. Support those in your team who tend towards big-picture thinking – incremental evolution needs to be balanced by big paradigm shifts sometimes.

11. Allow the naïve questions: just because conventional thinking is established, that doesn't mean that there isn't a different route.

12. Watch out for hard-working team members who need training or coaching in standing out.

13. Have time for your team's ideas. Accept that they may

not be in your language, and get to the core of the idea even if the format is difficult at first.

14. Don't have different rules for different people as far as funny is concerned. Don't allow the banter in the workplace to squeeze anyone into a corner.

15. Make sure that your introverted team members receive the same level of respect and attention as the louder extroverts demand.

16. Give your team clarity on your expectations of being managed as their boss. If their expectations of you and your all-knowingness are too high, then explain what they can expect and what you need from them.

17. Ensure that your whole team are expressing their real opinions. If everyone does as they are told all the time, then there is something wrong. It is all too easy to surround yourself with yes-men. It won't do you or the organisation any good in the long run.

18. Be sensitive to the different expectations of your team members and spend time with the ones you just don't 'get' instinctively. It will pay off.

19. Any boss needs to be flexible in how they deal with their team. If you aren't, don't expect everyone to like it or to put up with it.

20. A good manager ensures that everyone in the team feels welcome. If you have an exclusively barrack-room culture, you won't attract a range of great people.

21. As the boss, stand by your talented people whatever they get up to, but give them this to read.

22. One size doesn't fit all, and the investment in people will pay back in spades. Make sure people know that you're there to get the best from them and then DO IT.

23. As a company, regularly work on whether your company has an 'inclusive' culture. Ensure that you create the environment for talent to shine, rather than employ the same old types and then expect a different outcome.

24. As team leader, step in, restore confidence, move on.

25. As team leader, you need to diagnose what's going on and deal with it.

26. Make sure that you treat your talent as adults; if you have to say 'no', have a counter-offer.

27. Don't lose people because you have boxed them into a stereotype.

28. Make sure you are aware of the secret rules of your own organisation, and of who is playing games with them.

29. You should understand that the women in your team may not understand the numbers game as intuitively as the men.

30. Everyone needs a playbook.

31. Make sure that you balance the broad needs of the team with the needs everyone has from time to time for some personal praise or a private pat on the back.

32. Women are more likely to be conditioned to be agreeable in order to be liked. You might need to give the women who work for you permission to be pissed off and to draw the line.

33. Odd one out – this is a workplace culture issue. Don't let decisions be made when key members of the team are being excluded.

34. Are you overlooking a woman for promotion because she is less likely to ask for it? Listen to those third-party advocates. Seek out their views on your business. You

may find their objectivity is useful to you. Think about how you say 'no' to that woman if she does ask, so that you don't deter her ambition.

35. Obviously, you cannot run a business based on people's temper tantrums. However, the best decisions can sometimes come from disagreements, and it is always good to know what your team are passionate about and who really cares.

36. If team members have problems working through their disagreements, then some coaching may be necessary so that everyone can operate with the firm's best interests at heart for the long term.

37. Always on. The person you treat brusquely may be a brief forgotten encounter to you, but they will remember you. Always.

38. Mandate fairness in your middle managers' key performance indicators – they should know that it is crucial to their successful career progression to be fair to their teams, not just to deliver short-term results.

39. Make memory. If you break protocol as the boss, it will mean a huge amount to your team.

40. Pay it forward. Always do what you can, not just because it helps the business but because it will create the kind of atmosphere that everyone will benefit from, and the best people will hate to leave.

41. We're all human. We all need compassion when we are under stress. Set a standard of good intentions in the workplace.

ACKNOWLEDGEMENTS

The authors would like to thank everyone involved in the development of this book. So many of you have asked to remain nameless, it would be wrong to name names here. But we are very grateful to you all. It would have been impossible without your help.

Preface and Introduction

Books

Hook, P. (2013). *Breakfast at Sotheby's: An A–Z of the Art World.* Penguin.

Larouche, J., and Ryan, R. (1984). *Strategies for Women at Work.* Avon Books.

Papers and reports

Barsh, J., and Yee, L. (2012). *Unlocking the Full Potential of Women at Work.* McKinsey & Co. http://www.mckinsey.com/client_service/organization/latest_thinking/women_at_work

Catalyst (2007). 'Companies with More Women Board Directors Experience Higher Financial Performance'. http://www.catalyst.org/media/companies-more-women-board-directors-experience-higher-financial-performance-according-latest

Chanavat, A., and Ramsden, K. (2013). *Mining the Metrics of Board Diversity* [online]. Thomson Reuters. http://share.thomsonreuters.com/pr_us/gender_diversity_whitepaper.pdf

Clarke, C. (2013). 'Research Shows Profitable Companies Have More Women on Boards'. *Financial Times Online*, 25 July. http://www.ft.com/cms/s/2/2d320562-f52d-11e2-94e9-00144feabdc0.html#axzz3uaN21M7G

Department for Business, Innovation and Skills (2015). *Women on Boards: Davies Review Annual Report.* https://www.gov.uk/government/uploads/system/uploads/attachment_data/file/415454/bis-15-134-women-on-boards-2015-report.pdf

The Guardian Online (2014). *Women's Rights Country by Country. Guardian*, 4 February. http://www.theguardian.com/global-development/ng-interactive/2014/feb/04/womens-rights-country-by-country-interactive

KPMG and YSC (2014). *Cracking the Code*. https://www.kpmg.com/UK/en/IssuesAndInsights/ArticlesPublications/Documents/PDF/About/Cracking%20the%20code.pdf

McKinsey & Co. (2015). *The Power of Parity: How Advancing Women's Equality Can Add $12 Trillion to Global Growth*. http://www.mckinsey.com/insights/growth/how_advancing_womens_equality_can_add_12_trillion_to_global_growth

Swedish Corporate Governance Board (2013). *Annual Report*. http://www.corporategovernanceboard.se/media/62237/koll_arsrapport-2013_eng_20131002.pdf

1 Ambition

Books

Peter, L. J., and Hull, R. (1994). *The Peter Principle*. Souvenir Press.

Rumelt, R. (2011). *Good Strategy, Bad Strategy: The Difference and Why it Matters*. Profile Books.

Papers and reports

Adams, R., and Pearson, C. (2014). 'We Asked Women How They Really Feel About Ambition – This Is What They Had To Say'. *The Huffington Post*, 8 October. http://www.huffingtonpost.com/2014/10/08/women-ambition_n_5761784.html

Adams, Susan (2014). 'Women Lose Ambition Once They Get to Work', *Forbes*, 4 November. http://www.forbes.com/sites/susanadams/2014/11/04/women-lose-ambition-once-they-get-to-work/#21b7f5195679

Clark, N. F. (2014). 'Act Now to Shrink the Confidence Gap'. *Forbes*, 28 April. http://www.forbes.com/sites/

womensmedia/2014/04/28/act-now-to-shrink-the-confidence-gap/#2715e4857a0b66f942904509

Coffman, J., and Neuenfeldt, B. (2014). 'Everyday Moments of Truth: Frontline Managers Are Key to Women's Career Aspirations', Bain & Co. http://www.bain.com/Images/BAIN_REPORT_Everyday_moments_of_truth.pdf

Ernst and Young (2013). *From Elite Female Athletes to Exceptional Leaders*. http://www.ey.com/Publication/vwLUAssets/Elite_female_athletes_to_exceptional_leaders/$FILE/Elite%20female%20athletes%20and%20exceptional%20leaders%20Rio%20event.pdf

Fels, A. (2004). 'Do Women Lack Ambition?' *Harvard Business Review*, April. Available at: https://hbr.org/2004/04/do-women-lack-ambition

Riley, J. G., and Jones, R. B. (2007). 'When Boys and Girls Play'. *Childhood Education* 84(1).

2 Creativity

Books

Murray, D. K. (2010). *Borrowing Brilliance: The Six Steps to Business Innovation by Building on the Ideas of Others.* Random House Business.

Shlain, L. (1999). *The Alphabet Versus the Goddess.* Penguin Books.

Trott, D. (2015). *One Plus One Equals Three: A Masterclass in Creative Thinking.* Macmillan.

Papers and reports

Faccio, M., Mura, R., and Marchica, M. T. (2015). 'CEO Gender, Corporate Risk-Taking, and the Efficiency of Capital Allocation'. Social Science Research Network. http://ssrn.com/abstract=2021136

IPA (2014). '2014 Agency Census'. http://www.ipa.co.uk/news/ipa-publishes-2014-agency-census#.VqEXAJqLTct

Proudfoot, D., Kay, A. C., and Koval, C. Z. (2015). 'Gender Bias in the Attribution of Creativity'. *Psychological Science* 26(11), pp. 1751–61.

3 Cutting Through

Books

Cain, S. (2012). *Quiet: The Power of Introverts in a World that Can't Stop Talking*. Penguin.

De Beauvoir, S. (1949). *The Second Sex*. Translated by H. M. Parshley. Jonathan Cape Ltd, 1953. Reprinted, Vintage Classics, 1997.

Donne, J. (1990). *John Donne: The Major Works*. Edited by John Carey. Oxford University Press. Reprinted, 2008.

Drucker, P. (2007). *The Essential Drucker*. Routledge.

Jung, C. G. (1959). *The Archetypes and the Collective Unconscious*. Bollingen Foundation. Reprinted, Routledge, 1991.

Kay, K., and Shipman, C. (2014). *The Confidence Code*. HarperBusiness.

Sandberg, S. (2015). *Lean In*. W. H Allen.

Papers and reports

Opportunity Now (2014). *Project 28–40: The Report*, Business in the Community. http://gender.bitc.org.uk/system/files/research/project_28–40_the_report_2.pdf

Peters, T. (1997). 'The Brand Called You'. *Fast Company Magazine,* 31 August. http://www.fastcompany.com/28905/brand-called-you

The Atlantic (2010). 'Western, Educated, Industrialized, Rich, and Democratic'. 4 October. http://www.theatlantic.com/daily-dish/archive/2010/10/western-educated-industrialized-rich-and-democratic/181667/

Online resources

The Myers & Briggs Foundation. *Myers Briggs Personality Type Indicator.* www.myersbriggs.org

4 Trouble

Books

Burchill, J. (2013). *Ambition.* Corvus.

5 Resilience

Books

Babcock, L., and Laschever, S. (2008). *Why Women Don't Ask: The High Cost of Avoiding Negotiation – and Positive Strategies for Change.* Piatkus.

Scott-Morgan, P. (1994). *The Unwritten Rules of the Game: Master Them, Shatter Them, and Break Through the Barriers to Organizational Change.* McGraw-Hill.

Papers and reports

Henion, A., and Moser, J. (2014). 'Positive, Negative Thinkers' Brains Revealed'. Michigan State University. http://msutoday.msu.edu/news/2014/positive-negative-thinkers-brains-revealed/

Lipman, J. (2014). 'Women at Work: A Guide for Men'. *The Wall Street Journal,* 12 December. http://www.wsj.com/articles/women-at-work-a-guide-for-men-1418418595

Marcus, B. (2014). '7 Unwritten Rules of the Office Your Boss Will Never Tell You'. *Business Insider,* 28 August. http://www.businessinsider.com/unwritten-office-rules-your-boss-wont-tell-you-2014–8?IR=T

Online resources

Adaptiv Learning Systems. http://www.adaptivlearning.com/

VIA, *Character Strengths Survey.* www.viacharacter.org

6 Anger

Books

Machiavelli, N. (1532). *The Prince*. Translated by George Bull. Penguin Books, 1961. Reprint 2003.

Papers and reports

BBC Online (2009). 'Anger at Work "Good for Career"'. 2 March. http://news.bbc.co.uk/1/hi/health/7918622.stm

Derra, S. (2015). 'Study Shows Angry Men Gain Influence and Angry Women Lose Influence'. Arizona State University, 27 October. https://asunow.asu.edu/20151027-study-shows-angry-men-gain-influence-and-angry-women-lose-influence

Online resources

Cuddy, Amy (2012). *Your Body Language Shapes Who You Are*. [TED talk, Edinburgh] June. http://www.ted.com/talks/amy_cuddy_your_body_language_shapes_who_you_are#t-7454

7 Karma

Books

Albright, M. (2013). *Madam Secretary: A Memoir*. 2nd edn. Harper Perennial.

Campbell, J. (1968). *The Hero with a Thousand Faces*. Princeton University Press.

Kawasaki, G. (2012). *Enchantment: The Art of Changing Hearts, Minds and Actions*. Portfolio Penguin.

Stein, S. J. (2011). *The EQ Edge*. 3rd edn. Jossey-Bass.

Papers and reports

Kelly, C., Kocourek, P., McGaw, N., and Samuelson, J. (2005). *Deriving Value from Corporate Values*. Booz Allen Hamilton/Aspen Institute. https://www.aspeninstitute.org/sites/default/files/content/docs/bsp/VALUE%2520SURVEY%2520FINAL.PDF

APPENDIX

In summer 2015 Lightspeed GMI conducted new research into men and women's attitudes to work in the UK, the USA and Russia.

These are some of the key findings.

The feminine–masculine continuum

When asked to score themselves between 1 and 10 for their personal style at work (where 1 is highly feminine and 10 is highly masculine), significant proportions of women score themselves at 5 or higher: i.e., towards the masculine end of the spectrum (more than 30 per cent). Insignificant numbers of men score themselves at lower than 5: i.e., more feminine in style (less than 3 per cent). In the UK 35 per cent of women would score themselves at 5 plus; just 10 per cent of men at 5 or less. In the USA 23 per cent of women score themselves at 5 plus; 5 per cent of men at 5 or less. In Russia 40 per cent of women score themselves at 5 plus; no men in Russia score themselves at 5 or less.

As we wrote in the afterword, this is significant. There may be a divide between how you see yourself and how your boss sees you. Women are far more adaptable in style than men.

This is the picture across all three regions:

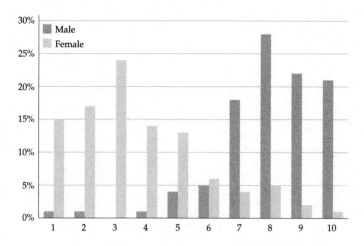

FIG 1

All regions: on a scale of 1 to 10 how masculine or feminine would you say you were?

And by region:

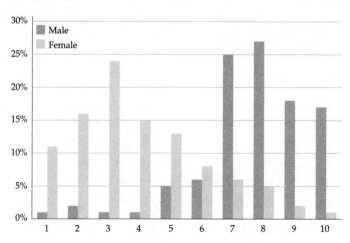

FIG 2

UK: On a scale of 1 to 10 how masculine or feminine would you say you were?

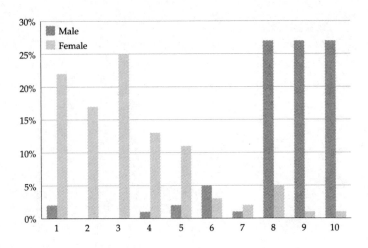

FIG 3
USA: On a scale of 1 to 10 how masculine or feminine would you say you were?

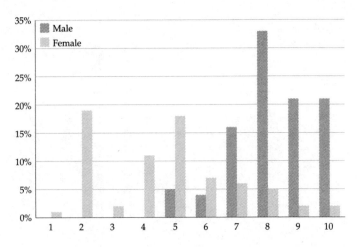

FIG 4
Russia: On a scale of 1 to 10 how masculine or feminine would you say you were?

Gender as a career barrier

At least a third of women surveyed have had experiences where they believe that they would have been more successful if they were men, especially in Russia.

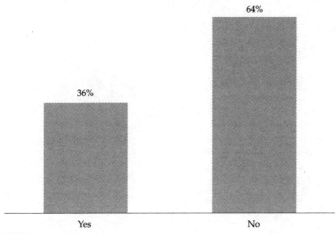

FIG 5

Have you ever felt that a situation has arisen in your career where you would have been more successful if you were a man?

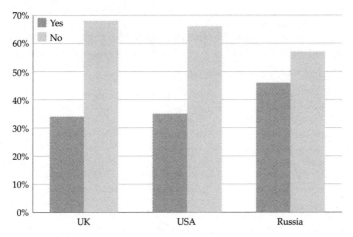

FIG 6

Have you ever felt that a situation has arisen in your career where you would have been more successful if you were a man?

Workplace barriers

Two-thirds of all respondents (women and men) think that women face barriers in the workplace that men do not.

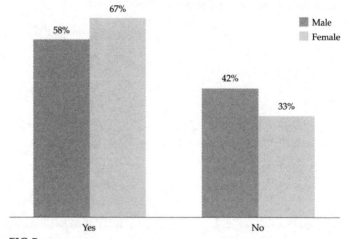

FIG 7
Overall do you think women face barriers to success in the workplace that men do not?

The overall figures would be even higher except for Russia. Here it is very different, with much less agreement by either men or women to this statement.

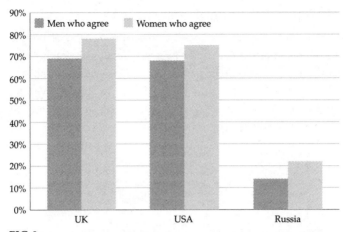

FIG 8

Overall do you think women face barriers to success in the workplace that men do not?

Barriers to success

Two-thirds of women surveyed say that they have experienced barriers to their career success.

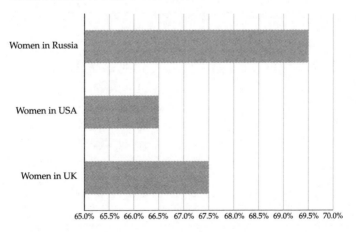

FIG 9

I've experienced significant barriers in my career (scoring 5+ on a scale of 1–10)

The effects of maternity or paternity leave

Our survey reveals that a substantial proportion of people who have taken maternity or paternity leave believe that this has affected their career progression. More than 40 per cent of women believe this, and a fifth of men (of course, far more women than men have taken a career break for parenting in the countries we have surveyed).

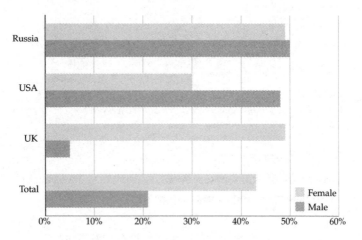

FIG 10
% who think that taking parenting leave has affected their career

Ambition

Overall men rate themselves as more ambitious than women, especially in the UK and Russia (but to a lesser extent in the USA).

All three countries:

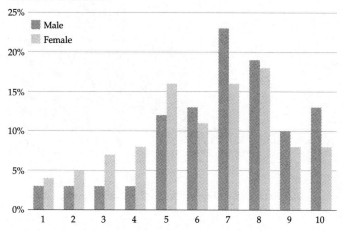

FIG 11
On a scale of 1 to 10 how ambitious would you say you were?

UK survey:

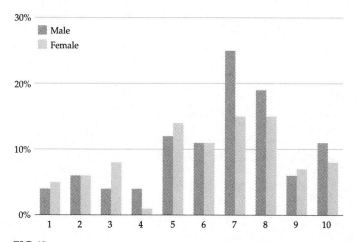

FIG 12
On a scale of 1 to 10 how ambitious would you say you were?

USA survey:

FIG 13
On a scale of 1 to 10 how ambitious would you say you were?

Russia survey:

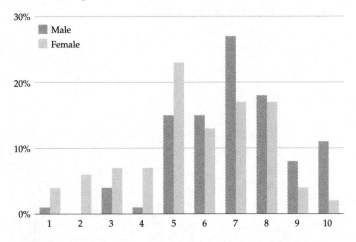

FIG 14
On a scale of 1 to 10 how ambitious would you say you were?

The wrong career

More than 40 per cent of women surveyed would like to reconsider their career choice; this is especially true in Russia.

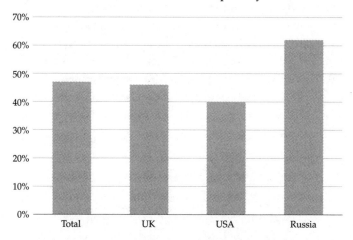

FIG 15
In retrospect would you change your choice of career?

Levelling the playing field

Only 6 per cent of respondents believe that nothing will change and that nothing can be done, while 10 per cent simply have no idea what could be done to improve things. Those who believe that change is a possibility provided some possible solutions. Several believe that more women in senior management will help to create change, and some call for complete equality in government as well as business. One respondent quoted the Chinese proverb 'The fish rots from the head' to call for the real change in attitude from the top. Many believe that existing managers must take responsibility for ensuring that there is no bias in hiring and promoting. Only a very few of those surveyed called for quotas. Several people said that men just need to give women a chance, to listen when they speak out and learn how to treat everyone (not just men) as human. The fact that paternity leave is so much less common or less extended than maternity leave was cited as an issue by some. Culturally there was a call for society to be aware that not only parental responsibility but also care for elderly relatives and dependants is often greater for women.

Many talked eloquently about the need for everyone in the workplace to be more aware of the many issues we examine in *The Glass Wall*.

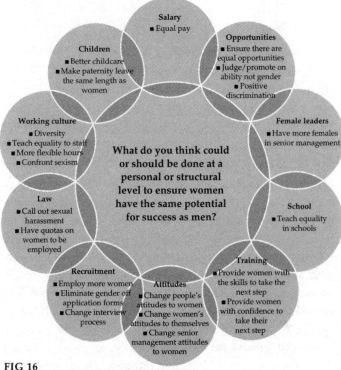

FIG 16

http://www.lightspeedgmi.com/

Copyright © 2015 Lightspeed LLC (Sample size: 1,165)
With special thanks to Mandy Pooler, Alex Wheatley, Martin Filz and Simonne Mason